EDITOR'S LETTER

A century of silencing dissent

The centenary of the Chinese Communist Party is no cause for celebration, says **MARTIN BRIGHT**, but its significance cannot be ignored

THIS SUMMER, THE Chinese Communist Party celebrates its 100th birthday. It does so at a moment when the West seems uncertain in its approach to an increasingly confident and aggressive Chinese brand.

In recent months we have seen growing international concern about the abuses of the Uighur population in Xinjiang Province and the crackdown on protesters in Hong Kong. Governments in Europe and the USA have expressed their horror, while knowing they cannot close the door to trade with the world's newest economic superpower. Index will not be celebrating the anniversary but it is important to mark it – especially as it coincides with a renewed crackdown on internal dissent and foreign journalists inside China. Earlier this year we witnessed the removal of the BBC World Service's licence to broadcast in response to a similar move by the UK regulator regarding Chinese state broadcaster CGTN. Veteran media commentator Ian Burrell writes for us about this media war and the distinction between independent national broadcasters and state-controlled propaganda outlets.

The centrepiece of our special report is a highly personal essay by Chinese-born British writer Ma Jian, who writes of his own teenage experience of the Great Famine – in which 45 million of his fellow citizens died – and his belief that the CCP and China are not one and the same.

He suggests an alternative Chinese culture based on Confucian principles of "benevolence, righteousness and propriety".

Former Index editor Rachael Jolley sets the context by talking to prominent historians studying China today. They suggest the Chinese tradition of censorship can be traced not just to Mao Zedong and the Cultural Revolution but further back to Sun Yat-sen, the first president of the Chinese republic, who believed his people were not ready for democracy.

China's desire to control the narrative of its global economic brand is the subject of a number of pieces, including Issa Sikiti da Silva's examination of China's economic influence in Africa

Contributing editor Kaya Genç looks at Turkey as it struggles with the geopolitical challenge represented by its Uighur refugees, and Stefano Pozzebon writes of the pressure placed on Paraguay to end its special relationship with Taiwan and switch allegiance to Beijing.

Meanwhile, Sally Gimson assesses how Chinese cultural colonialism reaches into the heart of British academia.

Technology is crucial to China's control of its people but, at the same time, it offers new possibilities of resistance. We talk to one of the founders of GreatFire which monitors Chinese state control of the internet and provides the means to circumvent the country's Great Firewall.

And Tianyu M Fang explains how young people's allegiance to the party

is being reinforced but also tested by digital technology.

While authoritarian regimes such as China still pose the greatest threat to free expression around the world, the big technology companies provide challenges of their own. Index trustee Sarah Sands, former editor of the Evening Standard and BBC Radio 4's Today programme, interviews Facebook vice-president Nick Clegg about how the company grapples with censorship issues. The former UK deputy prime minister tells how he was inspired by the revolutions that led to the end of the Cold War and how the optimism of those times has turned sour.

Index also takes pride in publishing the work of writers and artists themselves. In this edition you can read exclusive stories by American novelist Shalom Auslander and Syrian writer Khaled Alesmael, poetry by Ukrainian national hero Vasyl Stus, and lyrics by exiled Iranian singer Gelareh Sheibani.

Which brings us to our own anniversary. It is 50 years since the charity that established Index on Censorship was formed: a genuine cause for celebration.

The founders Stephen Spender, Elizabeth Longford, Stuart Hampshire and Peter Calvocoressi were dedicated to exposing the plight of writers working behind the Iron Curtain. Their anti-totalitarian approach inspired the work of the organisation as it expanded to campaign for those whose voices were being silenced around the world.

We continue that tradition with humility and pride. ⊛

Martin Bright is editor of Index on Censorship

50(01):1/1|DOI:10.1177/03064220211012277

Technology is crucial to China's control of its people but, at the same time, it offers new possibilities of resistance

CONTENTS

The Index

A round-up of events in the world of free expression from Index's unparalleled network of writers and activists

PICTURED: A protester takes shelter behind a rubbish bin adorned with an image of Myanmar armed forces chief Senior General Min Aung Hlaing during a demonstration against the military coup in Yangon in March 2021

The Index

PIONEER REPORTER

PATRICIA DEVLIN shares the story of Nellie Bly, an investigative journalist in the USA who went undercover in a lunatic asylum in the late 19th century and exposed the horrific conditions there

WAS A TEENAGE journalism student when I first discovered the magnificent Nellie Bly.

It was my first week at university in Northern Ireland and my tutor handed each person in our class a list of suggested books to read for the upcoming term.

When scouring the shelves of the campus library, I stumbled across Cupcakes and Kalashnikovs – a book which, 15 years later, I still pick up and flick through when I need inspiration.

Put together by the wonderful Eleanor Mills and Kira Cochrane, it is one of the first detailed collections of ground-breaking journalism by women over the past 100 years. It includes powerful pieces such as Martha Gellhorn's Dachau, Audre Lorde's haunting That Summer I Left Childhood Was White, and the late Ruth

> I found Nellie, a fierce female who trailblazed her way through newspaper journalism and paved the way for female investigative reporters around the world

Picardie's deeply emotive and last ever Observer column, Before I Say Goodbye.

It was in this anthology that I found Nellie, a fierce female who trailblazed her way through newspaper journalism and paved the way for female investigative reporters around the world.

Born Elizabeth Jane Cochrane in 1864, she began her career after her parents' deaths by writing a letter to the editor of the Pittsburgh Dispatch.

That letter – signed simply "Lonely Orphan Girl" – piqued George Madden so much, he immediately hired her.

Madden suggested she change her name to Nellie Bly, taken from a popular Stephen Foster song of the time, and the rest, as they say, is history.

From the moment she entered journalism, Nellie refused to conform.

Instead of writing about society gatherings and parties, a genre in which many women journalists were pigeonholed at that time, she sunk her teeth into social issues affecting women, from divorce laws to factory working conditions.

When working for The New York World in 1888, she feigned insanity to be committed into an asylum where she lived side by side with vulnerable women to expose the horrific, rat-infested and abusive conditions they were incarcerated in.

Her fearless piece, Ten Days in a Mad-House, led to the City of New York spending an extra $1 million a year on the care of those with serious mental health issues. She risked her freedom and her welfare for the truth.

Free speech in numbers

276
People considered as political prisoners in Belarus. Source: Viasna Human Rights Centre, 11 March

114,575,718
Views on YouTube of Alexei Navalny's exposé of "Putin's Palace" in the two months after it was posted in mid-January 2021.

392
Journalists who were assaulted in the US in 2020. Source: US Press Freedom Tracker

58.6%
Proportion of seats in the country's lower house won by Aung San Suu Kyi's National League for Democracy Party at Myanmar's November general election.

ABOVE: Pioneering female investigative journalist, Nellie Bly who wrote Ten Days in a Mad-House

She saw it as a small price to pay to highlight injustice, particularly for women who at that time didn't even have the right to vote.

Bly left journalism to get married and ran her husband's Iron Clad Manufacturing business. When it went bust she returned to journalism and filed stories from the Eastern Front during World War I. Bly was the first woman and one of the first foreigners to visit the war zone between Serbia and Austria. She was arrested when she was mistaken for a British spy. She died aged 57 in 1922.

It's been more than 100 years since Nellie Bly penned her last article, but the bravery, tenacity, and resilience she showed back then still inspires me today.

In her own words: "I said I could and I would. And I did."

Timeless. ⊗

Patricia Devlin is an award-winning journalist based in Ireland. She has persisted with her hard-hitting crime investigations despite threats and intimidation

You may have missed

BENJAMIN LYNCH rounds up important news on free expression from around the world

Lèse-majesté angst continues
43-YEAR SENTENCE SENDS THAILAND BACKWARDS AGAIN
Protests against the laws prohibiting criticism of the monarchy have continued after former civil servant Anchan Preelert was jailed for 43 years. The 65-year-old shared audio and video clips on social media. Her initial sentence of 87 years was halved after a guilty plea.

UK photographer arrested and fined
AN ALARMING ATTACK ON PRESS FREEDOM IN THE UK
Photographer Andy Aitchison was arrested at his home on 28 January after covering a protest at Napier Barracks, a Kent asylum seekers' camp.

His fingerprints were taken and his mobile phone and memory card were seized after he was held on suspicion of criminal damage

The case was dropped but Aitchison was later issued with a £200 fixed penalty fine for breaching Covid-19 rules. The police later said that fine had been issued erroneously.

Top radio broadcaster forced off air
ANOTHER OF VIKTOR ORBÁN'S CRITICS HAS BEEN SILENCED
On 9 February, Hungarian radio station Klubrádió was forced off the air and can now only broadcast online. It was one of the few remaining radio stations opposed to prime minister Viktor Orbán.

In 2018, Orbán told the European Parliament that "we would never sink so low as to silence those with whom we disagree".

Polish historians forced to apologise
HOLOCAUST RESEARCH COMES UNDER FIRE
Two historians were forced to apologise to the niece of a Polish former mayor after a co-authored book spoke of the complicity of some Catholic Poles during the Holocaust.

The Polish government had previously sought to criminalise any suggestion of Polish complicity in Nazi atrocities carried out in the country. ⊗

Drawing fire

BEFORE HE WAS arrested in May 2020, Bangladeshi cartoonist Ahmed Kabir Kishore chronicled the early days of the corona virus pandemic. His Life in the Time of Corona cartoons reflect Kishore's concerns about marginalised groups and the poorest in Bangladesh, as well as scepticism about the efficiency and parity with which PPE and vaccines would be distributed.

Kishore was eventually released from custody in March 2021. He described how, during his interrogation and torture at the hands of the police. His cartoons were projected on a screen. It seems the police were seeking to clarify whether any of the figures portrayed were intended to represent prime minister Sheikh Hasina or her father Sheikh Mujibur Rahman. It is considered a crime in Bangladesh under the 2018 Digital Security Act to make false statements about either political figure. Sheikh Mujibur Rahman was assassinated in 1975. ⊗

The Index

PEOPLE WATCH

JESSICA NÍ MHAINÍN highlights the stories of journalists imprisoned in Morocco and Belarus for reporting the news and a Lebanese filmmaker and critic of Hezbollah murdered in his car

Maâti Monjib

AFTER YEARS OF surveillance and harassment, the co-founder of the Moroccan Association of Investigative Journalism was convicted of fraud and of endangering state security in January and sentenced to a year in prison. As well as writing a weekly column for Le Journal, Monjib is a historian and human rights activist. The 60-year-old is currently on hunger strike.

Katsiaryna Barysevich

ON 2 MARCH, a Belarusian court sentenced the independent Tut.by journalist to six months in prison for disproving the authorities' account of the death of a protester, who died during an anti-regime demonstration last November. Barysevich used medical records to prove that the protester had died of severe injuries, widely believed to have been inflicted by police.

Andrei Aliaksandrau

FORMER INDEX STAFF member Aliaksandrau is a long-standing champion of free expression. He has written about the suppression of dissent in Belarus, Ukraine and Russia and the arrest and persecution of journalists. He was detained along with his partner, Irina Zlobina, in Minsk on 12 January on public order charges relating to protests against president Alexander Lukashenko.

Lokman Slim

FOLLOWING YEARS OF intimidation and threats, the filmmaker and human rights defender – who was a prominent critic of Hezbollah and other sectarian factions – was found dead in his car by Lebanese police. He had been shot four times in the head and once in the back. Many people including his sister accuse Hezbollah of the murder, but the group has denied being involved.

Cartoonists & Covid

TERRY ANDERSON, executive director of Cartoonists Rights Network International, says the pandemic has been used to crack down on satire

A YEAR IN, the picture is clear: human rights groups everywhere agree that the pandemic has provided a pretext for governments to advance authoritarian, populist and nationalist agendas. Indeed, last spring CRNI helped Index on Censorship's efforts to map violations by reporting multiple incidents of threat to cartoonists as part of Index's Disease Control? project.

Our network of cartoonists rated criminalisation as their chief anxiety prior to Covid-19. At the time of writing, cartoonists are at various stages of investigation or prosecution by national or regional governments in multiple locations; some are profiled in this issue. Our top priority is Ahmed Kabir Kishore, sorely abused by Bangladesh's police.

Additionally, the murder of teacher Samuel Paty in Paris last October has reintroduced the spectre of extremist violence to the wider conversation about cartooning. If a cartoon cannot be examined in an academic context then all hope is lost.

And in difficult days, the expression of dissatisfaction with power is the most natural human impulse. Cartoonists exemplify this, whether with the bluntest of caricatures or with the most nuanced of satirical allusions. We will continue to defend them. ✪

SPEAKING THE UNSPEAKABLE

As well as the magazine, Index produces content online. Here are the stories that have been the most read on our website

Loathsome but he's allowed to offend me

STEPHEN POLLARD, EDITOR of The Jewish Chronicle, wrote for Index after students at St Peter's College, Oxford, invited filmmaker Ken Loach to speak about his films and the Board of Deputies of British Jews weighed in, demanding that the invitation be withdrawn.

Pollard wrote: "Vile as I – and, let's be clear, many others – may find him to be, if a group of Oxford students wish to hear from Ken Loach, so be it. He has broken no laws when speaking and has as much right to put forward his views – and, of course, to talk about his films to a group of people interested in hearing from him about them – as anyone else."

Read the story: **tinyurl.com/Index501Loach**

Why Index is standing with Navalny

PUTIN RIVAL ALEXEI Navalny has been sent to a penal colony after being sentenced in a Russian court to two years and eight months in jail for violating parole – charges which Navalny's supporters say are trumped up.

However, Navalny has been criticised for his previous stance on immigration and racial slurs he has previously used, leading to some withdrawing their support for the dissident.

We wrote in March about Index's stance. "Index on Censorship was established to provide a voice for dissidents living either under authoritarian regimes or in exile. Throughout our history extraordinary people have written for us and we have campaigned for their freedom. Every time Index seeks to intervene there is obviously a consideration made about who we seek to shine a light on."

Read the story:
tinyurl.com/Index501Navalny

Our #JailedNotForgotten campaign

FOR OUR END-OF-YEAR campaign, we called on our readers to send messages of support to six activists or journalists who were in jail. We received hundreds of submissions wanting to pledge their support for Aasif Sultan (pictured), who was arrested in Kashmir after writing about the death of Buhran Wani; Golrokh Ebrahimi Iraee, jailed for writing about the practice of stoning in Iran; Hatice Duman, the former editor of the banned socialist newspaper Atılım, who has been in jail in Turkey since 2002; Khaled Drareni, jailed in Algeria for "incitement to unarmed gathering" simply for covering the weekly Hirak protests that are calling for political reform in the country; Loujain al-Hathloul, a women's rights activist known for her attempts to raise awareness of the ban on women driving in Saudi Arabia; and Yuri Dmitriev, a historian being silenced by Putin in Russia for creating a memorial to the victims of Stalinist terror and facing fabricated sexual assault charges.

Read the story:
tinyurl.com/Index501forgotten ⊗

The Index

World In Focus: Myanmar

Some 59 journalists have been arrested since the military coup on 1 February according to Reporting Asean. There are 28 still in detention. Many face charges under various sections of Myanmar's penal code which makes criticism of the military a crime

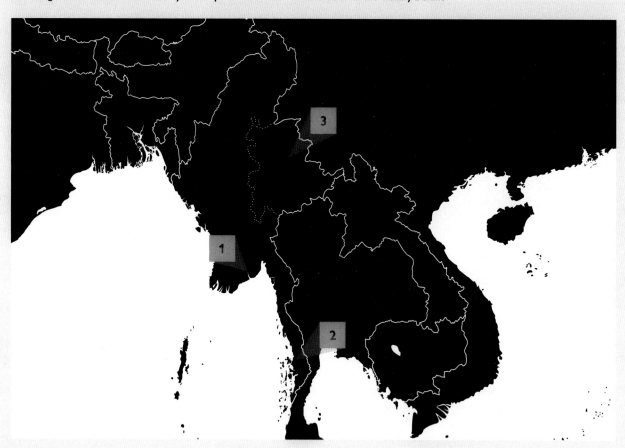

1 Yangon
Some 20 journalists have been arrested for covering protests in Yangon, according to the website Reporting Asean. Many were released shortly after, but Kay Zon Nway from Myanmar Now, Aung Ye Ko from 7Day, Ye Myo Khant from the Myanmar Pressphoto Agency, Hein Pyae Zaw from ZeeKwat Media, and freelance reporter Banyar Oo are still being held and have all been charged with incitement. AP photo-journalist Thein Zaw who was also charged was released after a hearing on 25 March 2021.

2 Myeik
Kaung Myat Hlaing (also known as Aung Kyaw) a reporter with the Democratic Voice of Myanmar (DVB), was targeted by police after reporting on anti-regime protests and how a pregnant woman in the city had been beaten up. The journalist live-streamed his own arrest in March which showed police and military surrounding his home, firing into the air and throwing stones at his house. The DVB news agency confirmed his detention in a statement and called for his release as well as the release of other journalists.

3 Shan State
Six journalists have been arrested in Shan over the last couple of months, but others have been attacked. A freelance reporter for the Shan Herald news agency, went to take photos of soldiers and found himself being assaulted by them. "They chased after him, and hit him in the chest with the barrel of a gun," said Sai Mun, an editor at the agency. "When he fell to the ground, they smashed the mobile phone he was taking photos with. They told him he couldn't take photos, and said he could be killed if he did." ✪

ASSANGE: FORGET WHAT YOU THINK YOU KNOW

MARK FRARY takes a look at stories that have generated the most interest on our Twitter channel. Follow us @IndexCensorship

JULIAN ASSANGE'S EXTRADITION trial in January meant that our social media channels were buzzing with news of the WikiLeaks founder. Our most popular tweet in the quarter related to Italian investigative journalist Stefania Maurizi's successful attempt to gain access to the full documentation held by various authorities related to the Assange and WikiLeaks cases via Freedom of Information legislation.

Our interview with Assange's partner Stella Moris and RSF's Rebecca Vincent (**tinyurl.com/Index501Moris**) also proved popular on Twitter. Moris told Index that people needed to "forget what they think they know" and assess the issues in her partner's case.

Our call to the Russian authorities to stop the harassment and prosecution of Sergey Smirnov, the editor-in-chief of independent Russian media outlet Mediazona struck a chord with our followers. Smirnov received 25 days of administrative arrest after retweeting a joke that mentioned a forthcoming anti-government protest.

Our call for messages of support for historian Yuri Dmitriev hit home too.

Dmitriev was jailed for three and a half years in 2020 on fabricated sexual assault charges after he annoyed Vladimir Putin by creating a memorial to the victims of Stalinist terror.

Yuri was one of six activists who were included in our 2020 year-end JailedNotForgotten campaign.

Another of the activists was award-winning journalist Aasif Sultan who has been detained in Kashmir for more than 800 days after writing about the death of the militant Buhran Wani.

In late December, Index wrote to United Nations Secretary–General António Guterres to protest the execution of journalist Ruhollah Zam (**tinyurl.com/ Index501Ruhollah**).

Our CEO Ruth Smeeth wrote, "On Saturday 12 December, a member of the UN General Assembly and a signatory of the Universal Declaration on Human Rights, the Islamic Republic of Iran, executed a journalist in cold blood, Ruhollah Zam. His apparent crime was 'corruption on Earth', or rather being a leading dissident against the Government."

Also engaging our followers on social media were our thoughts on the Scottish Government's Hate Crime and Public Order Bill. Our view (**tinyurl. com/Index501ScotHate**) was that the legislation had the potential to have a negative effect on freedom of expression in Scotland.

Rounding out our top ten tweets was a report from the NetBlocks observatory revealing that social media and messaging apps in Senegal had been disrupted after clashes between protesters and anti-riot police in Dakar following the arrest of opposition leader Ousmane Sonko. ⊗

Mark Frary is associate editor at Index

50(01):4/11|DOI:10.1177/03064220211012278

Tech watch

The innovations threatening freedoms around the world

A VIDEO OF a politician in an embarrassing situation goes viral. People on social media call for his resignation. But the video is a deepfake, footage that has been seamlessly and expertly manipulated to present something as real that is not.

Video editing technology that would once have been available only to Hollywood studios is now available on everyone's smartphone.

Deepfake Tom Cruise videos may seem like harmless fun but they are blurring the lines of reality.

In early 2020, India's Bharatiya Janata Party produced deepfakes of its president Manoj Tiwari. There was no sinister motive: it was just to show Tiwari speaking in the more than 20 different languages to appeal to more voters.

What is real? In February, a video appeared of a fitness instructor in Myanmar taking a class against a backdrop of a military coup. Was it a deepfake? Probably not, but no one could be sure.

With a deepfake app on your smartphone, it's quick and easy to embarrass your rivals. And if you get filmed making a shady deal? What then? Denounce it as a deepfake. Plausible deniability. ⊗

Fighting back against the menace of Slapps

JESSICA NÍ MHAINÍN reports on Index's campaign against the use of vexatious lawsuits to stifle free expression

ABOVE: Matthew Caruana Galizia, son of Daphne, and Rose Vella, Daphne's mother, attend a vigil in Malta's capital of Valletta, 2018

"THE TWO TIMES that me and my family left our home after my mother's death were, first, to identify my mother's remains in the morgue and, second, to go to a court hearing of the libel case brought by Chris Cardona against my mother," Andrew Caruana Galizia told a virtual audience at an event co-hosted by Index on Censorship in March.

"She was facing potential damages of millions of euros. After her death we found out she had been sued for $40 million in Arizona. If she hadn't been assassinated, the sad reality is she would have been completely crushed financially."

The 47 lawsuits that were pending against Maltese journalist Daphne Caruana Galizia at the time of her assassination constituted a vicious legal campaign aimed at depriving her of the time, money and energy she needed to continue exposing corruption at the heart of Malta's political establishment. These lawsuits were not filed in pursuit of judicial redress but to isolate, intimidate and ultimately stop her from publishing public interest investigations that were damaging to the interests of some of Malta's wealthiest and most powerful people. These kinds of lawsuits are known as strategic lawsuits against public participation (Slapps).

"Short of a gun to the head," one New York judge said of Slapps, "a greater threat to the First Amendment can scarcely be imagined." But as evidenced by Caruana Galizia's experience, the legal phenomenon is not confined to the USA, where the term originated in the 1980s. "Slapps have only relatively recently entered the English lexicon," explained Gill Phillips, director of editorial legal services at The Guardian, in a recent analysis of lawsuits. This is true not only of England but of Europe, where the acronym is now beginning to be used. "That is not to say that such lawsuits have not existed in the past, but that

If she hadn't been assassinated, the sad reality is she would have been completely crushed financially

there has been a slowness in attributing the Slapp label to them."

Addressing the lack of awareness of Slapps in Europe has been one of the key objectives of the Coalition Against Slapps in Europe (Case), which is made up of nearly 30 civil society organisations, including Index. Members of the coalition have been bringing cases to light in a bid to convince the European Commission – which is responsible for proposing new EU laws and policies – of the need to take action. Several Slapps uncovered and documented by Index have been among those brought to the commission's attention, including two ongoing cases outlined in Index's latest report, Slapped Down. The commission is now considering potential measures aimed at preventing Slapps.

"You could not have seen such activity in the previous commission, as the problem was not so visible and so urgent," said EU Commissioner Věra Jourová, who spoke alongside Andrew Caruana Galizia at the event in March. "What you are doing in the coalition is extremely useful to us. We will use your website as one of the tools of our work," she said, referring to the Slapp website that was launched by Case (the-case.eu) at the event. The website will serve as a repository for Slapp-related resources and information, including Index's reports, which will be useful to policymakers and those who may be facing Slapp threats or actions.

"You feel pretty alone when you get sued," Sara Farolfi, one of the journalists featured in Slapped Down, told Index last year. "There are not many people that understand why you – as a journalist – are undertaking that risk." She and her colleague, Stelios Orphanides, are being sued in Cyprus for up to €2 million by five Cypriot lawyers for a corruption investigation they published in 2018. "For them to file a lawsuit against two journalists, it just costs nothing. It just costs nothing. There are no downsides. They just need to do what they do every day. They don't need to allocate any

special resources to it. So there is this asymmetry – disproportion of forces."

Referring to the disparity of power and resources between claimant and defendant, Jourová said: "I always see it as a fight between David and Goliath." This imbalance is a hallmark of Slapps. Claimants will often exacerbate this, filing exaggerated claims that could never be recouped from the defendants. This is done to convince the target that they will lose everything if they don't succumb. Small investigative media outlets and freelance journalists are disproportionately affected, but individual journalists who work for larger organisations increasingly face individual lawsuits.

Anna Pihl and Mihkel Kärmas, who are also featured in Index's report, work as investigative journalists with Estonia Public Broadcasting (ERR), but they were sued individually for "up to €1 billion" by a Finnish businessman for an investigation that was broadcast and published online by ERR in 2018. "[Our employer] said that they will protect us and that we don't need to be personally responsible, whatever happens," Pihl told Index last year.

But the claimant nonetheless tried to force the journalists to pay for their own legal fees by preventing their employer from covering the costs. "[The claimants' lawyers] sent a letter to the parliament's culture commission, the finance ministry, the Estonian broadcasting's governing body and the state audit office asking whether they regard it appropriate use of public funds if the public broadcaster pays for our individual attorneys."

The claimants didn't succeed in making the journalists fund their legal defence, but what if they had done so? Pihl said she would have been afraid to publish further investigations about wealthy businesspeople. "That shouldn't be the case for a journalist," she said. Their case is ongoing.

"We all know that corruption scandals, political hypocrisy, fraud and other crimes see the light of day because journalists took risks and worked hard with their

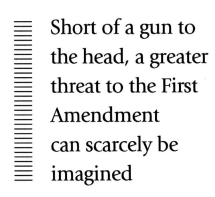

Short of a gun to the head, a greater threat to the First Amendment can scarcely be imagined

sources and with whistleblowers," Jourová said. "That's why there can be no healthy democracy without free, independent and pluralistic media. But media and journalists need to be protected so they can fulfil their crucial function."

That's why the commissioner has committed to proposing measures aimed at protecting Europe's journalists from Slapps later this year. Jourová would not be drawn on whether such an initiative would take the form of a directive, a regulation or a non-legislative measure but she said she "would prefer legally binding legislation".

A legally binding initiative would send a strong message of support to Europe's media which, according to Andrew Caruana Galizia, is desperately needed. "We need to find a way of not only supporting people who are being Slapped [but] even rewarding them for speaking out," he said. "Whistle-blowers, activists [and] journalists pay an enormous private cost for defending the public interest … My mother could have said, 'OK, this is a list of people I'm not going to write about because they are too dangerous or too wealthy', but she didn't."

How can we protect our democracy, our rule of law, our human rights if we cannot hold the powerful to account? We can't. Without the work of committed journalists, tyranny will prevail. ⊗

Jessica Ní Mhainín is the policy and campaigns manager at Index

50(01):12/13|DOI:10.1177/03064220211012279

what do we know and what should we do about...?

A collection of books that offer readers short, up-to-date overviews of key issues often misrepresented, simplified or misunderstood in modern society and the media.

immigration — Jonathan Portes

fake news

inequality

social mobility — Lee Elliot Major and Stephen Machin

internet privacy — Paul Bernal

housing — Rowland Atkinson and Keith Jacobs

sagepub.co.uk/WDWK

SAGE Publishing

FEATURES

The West has to be careful as it seeks to clip the wings of Silicon Valley companies...that it does not do so in a way which leaves the Chinese behemoths as the only untrammelled authority in the online world

NICK CLEGG SPEAKS TO SARAH SANDS | FRIENDLESS FACEBOOK P16

INTERVIEW

Friendless Facebook

SARAH SANDS talks to Nick Clegg, vice-president of the social media giant, about freedom of expression and whether clipping the wings of Silicon Valley entrepreneurs will leave the way open for domination by China

THE FOUNDING PRINCIPLE of Index on Censorship – freedom of expression – has become the democratic dilemma of our time. The instrument of people's power over tyrannical states – the internet – has itself become the subject of democratic disquiet.

Index came into existence, under the banner of Writers and Scholars International, with a response to a letter from Soviet dissidents. Stephen Spender wrote: "We, a group of friends representing no organisation, support your statement, admire your courage, think of you and will help in any way possible."

Whom should we, a group of friends representing no organisation, be helping now? Is it still just the silenced writers and scholars of Turkey, or China or the Russian opposition? Should we add to the list the former US president Donald Trump, whose Facebook account has been suspended indefinitely until a recently structured oversight board has pronounced judgment?

Amnesty International – an organisation entwined with Index, representing human rights as Index defends freedom of expression – has now taken a different course. It stripped Russian opposition politician Alexei Navalny of his prisoner-of-conscience status because of seemingly xenophobic comments he made in videos more than 10 years ago.

Index stood by its support of Navalny. And it appears now that the Russian government itself, in a classic smear campaign, was behind the many "complaints" which prompted Amnesty to act.

Is freedom of expression for only those with polite opinions? Above all, does power still lie with states or should we now fear the tech company behemoths which have become the arbiters of free speech?

Have we lost sight of the thrilling philosophy of Voltaire: "I disapprove of what you say, but I will defend to the death your right to say it"?

In the crosshairs of this debate is an English liberal, Nick Clegg, now vice-president for global affairs at Facebook. As leader of the Liberal Democrat party in the UK and then deputy prime minister, from 2010 until 2015, Clegg championed free speech. He managed to remove the offence of insulting speech from the Public Order Act. But is he now in the unhappy position of overseeing the greatest censorship of free speech since the Cold War?

Is there a new climate of authoritarianism, partly encouraged by the public itself? Political polarisation and public health seem to be the two causes – or justifications – for a tightening of the noose on free expression.

I speak via Zoom to Clegg at his home on the west coast of the USA and catch a wistfulness in his voice as he asks me about life in Norfolk, England. Clegg is truly a global citizen now and says that threats to free expression are springing up everywhere.

Governments want to regulate Facebook in order to challenge its colossal wealth and its power. Facebook may be a community of three billion users per month, but it feels strangely friendless.

Clegg wants to talk to Index because it is a return to his roots: "I am in my mid-50s and I am a liberal so I am, if you like, the archetype of someone for whom the collapse of the Berlin Wall and the end of the Cold War remain the most exhilarating and uplifting moments in my adult life.

"I was in a student flat in Minnesota when the Berlin Wall fell. I remember listening on the radio and just bursting into tears. It was just this extraordinary sense that millions of human beings and many wonderful accomplished intellectuals had been trampled underfoot by this ideology for so long, and literally from one moment to the next they were able to breathe.

"So what Index represents for my generation is this very brave and steadfast faith in the wonder of self expression and the wonder of open, raucous, uncontrolled self expression and intellectual self expression."

That was the dawn of free expression

> I get shouted out by irate Scandinavian politicians because Facebook doesn't allow nudity on its platform. It is a private company; if you use Facebook, you can't start flashing your genitals and your nipples

in the former Soviet Bloc, but has it survived the cold light of day? What would Vaclav Havel, the Czech dissident, writer and president from 1993 to 2003, make of the modern world?

Clegg believes that the dream of freedom of expression has curdled. "It certainly hasn't panned out the way we all dreamed that it would after the collapse of the Cold War. As for freedom of expression, it has become so much more complicated, because on one hand technology has erupted to emancipate and empower people in a way that never existed before and yet in many ways the pushback against free expression is just as serious as it was then."

He sees the threats from different directions and cites them with a degree of self-interest.

First, authoritarian governments are still "clobbering the rights of free individuals to say what they like". Clegg spends days resisting requests from Russia or Vietnam to take down Facebook content. But it is the power of China which makes even Facebook quake. He ruefully cites former US president Bill Clinton's prediction that the Chinese Communist Party could not survive the open technology of the internet.

"No one could have expected them to have been as devastatingly effective as they have been towards the internet, including fostering many companies which may rival and surpass the companies in Silicon Valley.

"They have built a wall round their citizens and carry out heavy surveillance of their citizens on the internet."

It is perhaps not surprising that the successor to the Berlin Wall should be virtual.

But should we entirely trust the superpower of Silicon Valley? Facebook enrages traditional media because it destroyed their economic model. It both enthrals and infuriates governments, which see it as a tax haven in the cloud.

The EU Digital Services Act intends to rein in the power of Facebook. The US Federal Trade Commission and 48 state

ABOVE: Nick Clegg believes the dream of freedom of expression has curdled

attorneys-general would like to see the monopolies broken up. Is it right that Facebook should also own Instagram and WhatsApp?

Clegg thinks we are missing the far greater threat. "The West has to be careful... as it seeks to clip the wings of Silicon Valley companies, which is understandable and laudable - all success and power should be held to account - that it does not do so in a way which leaves the Chinese behemoths as the only untrammelled authority in the online world."

The other threat to freedom of expression is harder to spot but perhaps more dangerous because it comes cloaked in good intentions. Freedom of expression can be rude and unkind. Cambridge University last year rejected new guidelines demanding that opinions should be "respectful". Atheists, in particular, asked why they should feign respect for views they considered absurd?

Much trickier issues for freedom of speech are things such as the UK's Online Harms Bill, which seeks to remove

material related to child sexual abuse and terrorism. The incitement-to-public-harm principle – the bedrock of Facebook's own content standards – looks watertight to Clegg, but he warns against mission creep.

"Society needs to be reassured that new technologies are there to serve society, not society to serve technology – but as democracies regulate, they should tread with care, act with precision and avoid making incursions into first order issues of free expression."

He cites Germany as an example of heavy-handed incursions. "Look at legislation on the statute book in Germany, one of the world's leading democracies. It is now illegal to maliciously gossip about people and insult people in certain circumstances."

The demand that public discourse should be kind has also come from Prince Harry, Duke of Sussex, who blames social media for inciting false information and hate speech.

Clegg sighs. "I don't want to start arguing with Prince Harry, but I am afraid freedom means there is freedom ➔

I don't want to start arguing with Prince Harry, but I am afraid freedom means there is freedom for good people to say good things but unfortunately it also means freedom for bad people to say bad things

→ for good people to say good things but unfortunately it also means freedom for bad people to say bad things. You can't eliminate the dark side of human nature.

"If you listen to people like Prince Harry, you'd think Facebook is just awash with hate speech. It's just simply not correct. The prevalence of hate speech on Facebook is 0.1 per cent of all content. I wish it were zero but we will never get it down to zero.

"It's right for people like Prince Harry to put pressure on companies like Facebook to enforce their rules, but let's not pretend that you can cleanse the world of people saying ugly things. You can't. You can't do so in a way that is compatible with the most elementary understanding of what a free society means."

Clegg points out that most of Facebook is exchanges of family and community content. He makes a good point on percentages, although it's important to bear in mind this is a percentage of a colossal amount of content.

Facebook says that it is looking for "rules of the road" and is happy to negotiate regulations with the world's democracies, but national differences may defy global rules.

Clegg, for instance, has fallen out with Scandinavia over nudity.

"I get shouted out by irate Scandinavian politicians because Facebook doesn't allow nudity on its platform. It is a private company; if you use Facebook, you can't start flashing your genitals and your nipples."

A debate with no end in sight

MARK FRARY finds that out of the 220,000 cases referred to Facebook's oversight board only six have so far been resolved

IS A SOCIAL network a platform that is not responsible for what its users post, or is it a publisher that makes decisions about what to allow?

An executive order made in May 2020 by then US president Donald Trump revealed his views on the subject. In the order, he wrote: "Twitter, Facebook, Instagram and YouTube wield immense, if not unprecedented, power to shape the interpretation of public events; to censor, delete or disappear information; and to control what people see or do not see."

The order aimed to clarify the scope of Section 230(c) of the Communications Decency Act, which provides some immunity to online platforms over what users post.

The order added: "Immunity should not extend beyond [Section 230(c)'s] text and purpose to provide protection for those who purport to provide users a forum for free and open speech, but in reality use their power over a vital means of communication to engage in deceptive or pretextual actions stifling free and open debate by censoring certain viewpoints."

Trump's argument was that if a social media company restricted access to some of its content then it would stop being a platform and instead become a "publisher" of all the content posted on its site, and therefore could be held responsible for defamation and other torts.

Facebook was quick to criticise the order in a statement saying: "Facebook is a platform for diverse views. We believe in protecting freedom of expression on our services, while protecting our community from harmful content including content designed to stop voters from exercising their right to vote. Those rules apply to everybody.

"Repealing or limiting Section 230 will have the opposite effect. It will restrict more speech online, not less. By exposing companies to potential liability for everything that billions of people around the world say, this would penalise companies that choose to allow controversial speech and encourage platforms to censor anything that might offend anyone."

The order came despite Facebook earlier that month naming the first members of a new independent oversight board.

The board's purpose, according to its establishing charter, is to "protect free expression by making principled, independent decisions about important pieces of content and by issuing policy advisory opinions on Facebook's content policies".

A minimum of 11 members, each serving a three-year term, make up the board but the size will fluctuate. Facebook believes the board is likely to have 40 members at any given time. It currently includes Yemeni Nobel Peace Prize laureate Tawakkol Karman, Internet Sans Frontières executive director Julie Owono and Colombian human rights lawyer Catalina Botero Marino.

The board started work in October 2020, allowing users whose content had been removed and who had exhausted Facebook's existing procedures to appeal. Decisions made by the board are binding on the company.

Since then, more than 220,000 cases have been appealed to the board. It says it cannot hear every appeal so it is prioritising cases that have the potential to affect lots of users around the world, are of critical importance to public discourse or raise important questions about Facebook's policies.

At the time of going to press, the board has made six decisions in cases that stretch around the world.

In one case, a user in Myanmar posted about a Syrian toddler of Kurdish ethnicity who drowned attempting to reach Europe in September 2015. The text of the post

"They say, 'It's what we do! Why are you being so prudish, you North Americans who have a higher tolerance for violence but a lower tolerance for nudity?'"

Facebook is under increasing pressure to regulate, and it appears more willing to do so. It would quite like to see the scrutiny and decision-making move elsewhere. Clegg seems grateful for the absolute powers of the oversight board, a board that includes figures such as former Guardian editor Alan Rusbridger and former Danish prime minister Helle Thorning-Schmidt (see below).

He is happy to negotiate with national governments over subjects such as privacy. At the moment the UK Home Secretary Priti Patel is on the warpath over end-to-end encryption, which she calls "morally wrong and dangerous", because it could give cover to paedophiles. Facebook owns WhatsApp. Clegg, in his former life as Liberal Democrat leader, fought home secretaries over incursions on civil liberties, but he seems meeker now.

"It is the age-old tension between privacy and security. It is one of the ancient debates in any democracy... It is not right for a private sector company to take all these decisions by itself. Facebook, since I arrived two years ago, has been saying that we need some rules of the road.

"There are aspects of regulation that we quibble with but, for instance, on encryption, we strongly believe in the privacy encryption brings. But Priti Patel is elected and we are not, so she will have to make her own decisions."

Facebook's willingness to hand over responsibility for regulating free speech to governments may get the company off the hook so that it can fight on the other front – that of governmental suppression of Facebook's great wealth.

The Australian government caused a diplomatic ruction recently by suggesting Facebook should subsidise media publishers. Facebook retaliated by threatening to pull out of Australia. The two sides achieved a truce of sorts, which probably leaves Facebook in the stronger position. Advertising revenues have moved voluntarily from newspapers to Facebook.

The question is whether the public service of verified news reporting should have a recognised value. The mainstream media say that Facebook takes all the gains without doing the work. Facebook ➜

suggested that "something's wrong with Muslims psychologically".

Facebook removed the post because its rules on hate speech prohibit generalised statements of inferiority about the mental deficiencies of a group on the basis of their religion.

However, the board overturned the decision, concluding that "while some may consider the post offensive and insulting towards Muslims, the board does not consider its removal to be necessary to protect the rights of others".

Of the six cases on which the board has ruled, it has overturned Facebook's decision to remove content in five of them.

In the case where Facebook's decision was upheld, a user posted content that included historical photos described as showing churches in Baku, Azerbaijan. The accompanying text in Russian claimed that Armenians built Baku and that this heritage, including the churches, had been destroyed.

The user used the term тазики ("Taziks") to describe Azerbaijanis, who the user claimed were nomads and had no history compared with Armenians.

The board said that while the term can be translated literally from Russian as "wash bowl", it can also be understood as wordplay on the Russian word "азики" ("aziks"), a derogatory term for Azerbaijanis, which features on Facebook's internal list of slur terms. The board said it was "a dehumanising slur attacking national origin".

Yet what may prove to be its most difficult decision related to events that took place in January when Trump was banned from Facebook after protesters stormed the US Capitol.

The ban came about as a result of posts made by Trump. One post, made while police were securing the Capitol, read: "These are the things and events that happen when a sacred landslide election victory is so unceremoniously and viciously stripped away from great patriots who have been badly and unfairly treated for so long. Go home with love and in peace. Remember this day forever!"

This and another post were removed as a result of Facebook's policy that prohibits praise, support and representation of events that Facebook designates as "violating" Facebook's policies.

Facebook founder Mark Zuckerberg said at the time: "We believe the risks of allowing the president to continue to use our service during this period are simply too great."

ABOVE: Yemeni journalist and human rights activist Tawakkol Karman, who is a member of Facebook's oversight board

Facebook has now asked the board to rule on the question of whether the decision to ban Trump was the right one.

Whichever decision the board makes, the question of whether Facebook is a platform or a publisher is likely to run and run. ⊗

Mark Frary is associate editor at Index

→ says that publishers benefit from the distribution of their material and news is a very small percentage of content.

As Facebook fights accusations of hubris, it still has to come to terms with the implications of its decision to censor Trump. It was the moment that the whole of tech – content and infrastructure – acted as one.

How hard a decision was it for a lifelong liberal such as Clegg to censor the president of the USA? "Oddly enough, it was a relatively clear-cut case, because it was such an obvious violation of the foundational principle that it does not matter who you are, you cannot use your megaphone to incite violence.

"What was interesting was that in the wake of that you had the gatekeepers of the internet infrastructure – Apple, Amazon, Google – basically unplugging a whole bunch of apps. It is the equivalent of if you had some violent heckler in the room, Facebook, Twitter and YouTube [are] saying 'Leave the room', and then the big guys who really

> Of course I believe in a democracy of ideas. The pendulum has swung from ludicrous tech euphoria, naivety, utopia, in which people like Steve Jobs and Mark Zuckerberg were treated like Mick Jagger

run the internet [are] basically cutting off the gas and electricity."

For many, that moment was a celebration. It was the literal taking down of a president whom many regarded as a tyrant.

But those who champion freedom of expression are left uneasy. Next Facebook is going after the anti-vaxxers, on the same principle of public harm. How will Facebook handle blood-curdling political rhetoric in other countries in the future?

On Navalny Clegg is clear that free speech is necessary: "Believing in free expression isn't always comfortable – it means allowing people to make their voice heard even when you or I may disagree strongly with what they have to say. Facebook draws the line at hate speech and content that causes harm, but otherwise we believe that people should be able to make their voice heard." But on the question of Myanmar he says the authorities there are abusing the platform.

"So we have been on high alert to stop that happening again. The military coup, combined with the Tatmadaw's history of severe human rights abuses and repeated violations of our policies, meant the risk of allowing them to continue using our apps is too great. Our commitment to free expression doesn't mean that those in power can use our tools to cause harm." But how can you tell the moment when rhetoric translates into deeds?

No wonder Facebook would rather share some of this regulatory decision-making. It is an epoch-forming moment when a tech company like Facebook gives up its rights to the First Amendment of the US Constitution. Clegg quickly points out the constitutional protection of free expression was aimed at governments rather than private companies. But what happens when private companies are more powerful and much richer than some governments?

I ask Clegg a final question. Does he still believe, in his heart of hearts, in the

ABOVE: Russian opposition leader Alexei Navalny during his trial in February 2021

democracy of ideas, or is there instead a corporate liberal consensus which threatens to monopolise expression?

"Of course I believe in a democracy of ideas. The pendulum has swung from ludicrous tech euphoria, naivety, utopia, in which people like Steve Jobs and Mark Zuckerberg were treated like Mick Jagger, like rock stars, who could do no wrong and who were the solution to all our problems.

"Now it is has swung completely the other way to a sort of hysterical view that it is all about data gouging, profiteering and the peddling of extremism deliberately stoked by some sort of reptilian algorithm. Neither is correct. I think if we can balance rights with regulation and accountability we can put this to rest and start to celebrate the good stuff. This is the biggest emancipation of self-expression since the printing press."

He still sounds like a liberal. ⊗

Sarah Sands is Chair of the Gender Equality Advisory Council for G7 and a board member of Index on Censorship

50(01):16/20|DOI:10.1177/03064220211012280

ABOVE: Former Ecuadorian president Rafael Correa holds up an oil-covered hand and calls for a boycott of Chevron, 2013

Standing up to a global oil giant

STEVEN DONZIGER faces yet another court appearance in the latest chapter of his long-running battle with Chevron

N FEBRUARY 2011, a court in Ecuador delivered a historic victory for indigenous and rural communities in that country's Amazon region: a multi-billion-dollar pollution judgment designed to remedy decades of deliberate toxic dumping by global oil company Chevron on indigenous ancestral lands.

I was a member of the international legal team that obtained the judgment after Chevron had insisted the trial take place in Ecuador. Since then, I have been targeted by the company with what can only be described as a vicious retaliation campaign against me and my family – a campaign designed to silence my advocacy and intimidate other human rights lawyers who might think of taking on the fossil fuel giants.

The evidence against Chevron, as found by Ecuador's courts, was overwhelming. It consisted of 64,000 chemical sampling results reporting extensive oil pollution at hundreds of oil production sites. Billions of gallons of toxic "produced water" were deliberately discharged into rivers and streams that locals relied on for their drinking water, fishing and bathing. Cancer rates in the region have spiked dramatically.

One experienced engineer who had worked on oil operations in dozens of countries told an energy journalist it was the worst oil pollution he had ever seen. When the indigenous people complained, the company's engineers told them that oil was like milk and that it contained vitamins.

At the time we won the judgment, I was living in Manhattan with my wife and young son in a small apartment. I was travelling to Ecuador on a monthly basis to help the affected communities while maintaining a small law practice.

To keep the litigation going, I helped my clients raise significant funds ➔

Chevron's counterattack targeting me came swiftly

→ from supporters and I helped recruit and manage attorneys from around the world who were preparing to enforce the winning judgment. Enforcement of the judgment became necessary after Chevron vowed never to pay and threatened the indigenous peoples who won the case with a "lifetime of litigation" unless they dropped their claims.

Chevron's counterattack targeting me came swiftly. In 2009, the company had hired a new law firm that broadly advertised a "kill step" strategy to help rescue corporations plagued by scandal from legal liabilities. This primarily involved accusing the lawyers who won a judgment against the firm's client of "fraud" to distract attention from the company's wrongdoing. The ultimate goal was to drive lawyers off the case by demonising them and making life so uncomfortable that their careers were at risk; under such a scenario, the victims of the company's pollution would be left defenceless.

In my case, Chevron lawyers sued me under a civil "racketeering" statute – accusing me of authorising the bribing of a judge in Ecuador. This is something I have not done, nor would I ever do.

The civil lawsuit was crafted by the Chevron lawyers to read like a criminal indictment. When it was filed in New York in 2011, my life was turned upside down. The company claimed the entire case I had been working on in Ecuador since 1993 was "sham" litigation even though Ecuador's courts had validated the pollution judgment based on voluminous scientific evidence. Chevron also sued me for $60 billion, the largest potential personal liability in US history. When I refused to give up, the company convinced a US judge in 2018 to charge me with criminal contempt of court for appealing an order that I turn over my electronic devices, passwords and confidential case file to the company.

At the time of writing, I have been under house arrest in Manhattan for roughly 600 days on a petty charge that carries a maximum sentence of just 180 days in prison. I am being prosecuted by a Chevron law firm in the name of the public after the charges were rejected by the regular federal prosecutor.

To monitor my whereabouts on a 24/7 basis, the court shackled my left ankle with a GPS monitor. It never comes off — I sleep with it, eat with it and shower with it. It often beeps in the middle of the night when the battery runs low.

In all, Chevron has used the US court system to subject me over the past 10 years to multiple attacks:

• Chevron paid an Ecuadorian witness at least $2 million. It also flew him and his entire family to the USA where they were settled in a new house. Chevron lawyers then coached this person for 53 days to be its star witness. He testified I approved a bribe of the trial judge in Ecuador. This was the "kill step" in action: I was falsely

The lawyer and the multi-billion dollar oil company

INDEX looks at how Texaco and Chevron became involved in Ecuador and the twists and turns of Steven Donziger's campaign to get compensation for local people

1964: Texaco begin oil exploration and drilling in Ecuador.
1992: Texaco hand over full control of the oil operation in the country to state-owned oil company PetroEcuador.
1993: Steven Donziger and his team file a suit against Texaco in New York, but Texaco successfully lobby to have the case heard in Ecuador.
1995: A settlement agreement is reached and Texaco agree to help with the clean-up of toxic waste.
1998: The clean-up costs $40 million and Ecuador releases another agreement stating Texaco had met its obligations under the 1998 agreement.
2000: Chevron buy Texaco for around $35 billion.

2003: A US legal team including Steven Donziger sues Texaco on behalf of over 30,000 Ecuadoreans, claiming that between from 1971 to 1992, Texaco dumped four million gallons of toxic wastewater per day.
2011: In February, Chevron sues Donziger and co. under the Racketeer Influenced and Corrupt Organizations Act (RICO), alleging extortion.
The original suit, the monetary claims of which were dropped before the trial, saw Chevron seeking $60 billion in damages.
2011: An Ecuadorean court gives a judgment for Chevron to pay $18 billion, which is later raised to $19 billion, to plaintiffs. Chevron appeal the decision.
2013: Ecuador's Supreme Court upholds the decision but halves the damages to $9.5 billion.

2014: US District Judge Lewis Kaplan rules the decision to be tainted and accuses Donziger of perverting the course of justice. Six other courts rule the decision to be valid. Much of the decision was based on the testimony of former Ecuador judge Alberto Guerra, who claimed there was bribery involved in the 2011 judgement. Parts of this testimony have since been retracted.
2018: Donziger is suspended from practising as an attorney.
2019: Kaplan charges Donziger with contempt of court and orders him to pay $3.4 million in attorney fees.
2020: In August, Donziger is disbarred. 29 Nobel laureates condemn alleged judicial harassment by Chevron.

being accused of a crime to ruin my career and remove me from the case. The witness later recanted much of his testimony, but the judge in the case denied me a jury of my peers and used the testimony to rule the Ecuador judgment was obtained by fraud and that I could not collect my legal fee.

- Chevron used these so-called findings of fact – findings contradicted by six appellate courts in Ecuador and Canada that rejected the company's false evidence – to orchestrate the suspension of my licence in New York without a hearing. I later won my post-suspension hearing; the case is currently on appeal.

- Chevron launched a series of financial attacks against me and my family. Even though the company had denied me a jury (required by law in damages cases), the judge allowed Chevron to impose draconian financial penalties on me to "repay" the company for some of the legal fees it used to prosecute me. The judge also imposed billions of dollars of fines on me for supposedly failing to comply with discovery orders that I had appealed. He also authorised the company to freeze my personal accounts and take my life savings.

- In the ultimate coup de grace, Chevron convinced the judge to essentially block me from working on the case by issuing an injunction preventing me from helping my clients raise investment funds to help enforce the judgment against Chevron's assets. The cold reality is that Chevron, which grosses about $250 billion a year, is free to spend what it wants to block enforcement actions brought by the Ecuadorian communities. The indigenous people of Ecuador, nmost of whom cannot afford even bottled water, are barred by US courts from raising money to enforce their judgment. The US court did say they could receive "donations", which will never be enough to cover the costs.

- In any criminal contempt case, no

Chevron hits back

SEAN COMEY, senior corporate adviser, Chevron Corporation, sent Index this response

Steven Donziger continues to try to shift attention away from the facts. In his own words, "we need to make facts that help us and the facts we need don't always exist".

The facts are that Donziger has been disbarred because of a pattern of illegal activity related to the case. Decisions by courts in the USA, Argentina, Brazil, Canada and Gibraltar and an international tribunal in The Hague confirm that the fraudulent Ecuadorian judgment should be unenforceable in any court that respects the rule of law. The US District Court for the Southern District of New York held that the judgment against Chevron was the product of fraud and racketeering, finding it unenforceable in the USA. The court found Donziger violated the US racketeering statute by committing extortion, wire fraud, money laundering, obstruction of justice, witness tampering and Foreign Corrupt Practices Act violations. The judgment is final after been unanimously affirmed by the Court of Appeals and denied review by the Supreme Court.

Even the government of Ecuador now acknowledges the judgment was based on fraud. The international Bilateral Investment Treaty tribunal in The Hague – including an arbitrator appointed by the Ecuadorian government – unanimously ruled the Ecuadorian judgment was based on fraud, bribery and corruption, and rejected the environmental allegations against Chevron, ruling those claims were settled and released by the Republic of Ecuador decades ago following an environmental remediation supervised and approved by the government.

person charged with a petty crime in the federal system has served even one day's pre-trial in-home detention; I have served almost two years without trial.

My trial on the six criminal contempt counts is scheduled for 10 May. All the counts relate to legitimate discovery disputes I had with Chevron that I was litigating at the time the judge charged me criminally. At the time, I was in Canada helping lawyers there enforce the Ecuador judgment.

I am a human rights lawyer who has received significant public support, including from 55 Nobel laureates who have demanded dismissal of the criminal case and my release. Thousands of prominent lawyers around the world, including Harvard professor Charles Nesson and legendary civil rights lawyer Martin Garbus, have rallied on my behalf. Courts around the world have validated the judgment I worked years to help secure. Yet Chevron, working through its 60 law firms and hundreds of lawyers, has effectively weaponised the judicial system in service of its interests to nullify my ability to fully function as an advocate. This has happened in retaliation for our success, not because of any errors along the way.

The victims of this new corporate playbook are the people of Ecuador; its higher purpose is to protect a fossil fuel industry that is destroying our planet from being held accountable under the law. The racketeering is the conspiracy organised by Chevron and its allies not only to "win" the case and extinguish the company's liability but also to kill off the idea that this type of environmental human rights case can happen again. It is critical that environmental justice lawyers, campaigners and all who believe in free speech stand up for the important principles so central to the proper functioning of a free society that are contained in this saga. ⊗

Steven Donziger is a US lawyer under house arrest in New York

50(01):21/23|DOI:10.1177/03064220211012281

Fear and loathing in Belarus

Since protests erupted over the re-election of Alexander Lukashenko, journalists like **LARYSA SHCHYRAKOVA** and **YAUHEN MERKIS** have borne the brunt of the government crackdown

ABOVE: Larysa Shchyrakova reporting from the protests in Belarus in 2020

N 2020, **477** journalists were detained in Belarus. Some 160 of them were held in a single month, August, when Alexander Lukashenko claimed a disputed victory in the country's elections. This gave the man who has been called "Europe's last dictator" a sixth term as president.

More than 60 of those journalists were subjected to violence, collectively faced more than 1,200 days in jail and were fined the equivalent of about $25,000.

This trend has continued into 2021. According to the Belarusian Association of Journalists, more than 50 journalists have been detained, been attacked or had their equipment stolen, including our former staff member Andrei Aliaksandrau.

Here, two journalists in Belarus talk of their own experiences of working in the country and the threats they have faced just for doing their job.

Larysa Shchyrakova
IS A FREELANCE JOURNALIST AND SINGLE MOTHER FROM GOMEL

I am 47 years old and a historian by education. But for the last 13 years I have been working as a journalist for the Belsat TV channel and the human rights website Gomel Spring. I shoot videos, take photos and write articles.

The repression against me began long before the disputed August presidential election, which Alexander Lukashenko said he won convincingly.

Since 2016, I have been in court some

45 times for working for the Belsat TV channel without accreditation from the Ministry of Foreign Affairs. The channel's management has repeatedly applied to the Ministry of Foreign Affairs for accreditation for its employees, but we have been denied.

In 2017, there were mass protests in Belarus against the unemployment tax, a "law against social parasites" proposed by Lukashenko's government that required people working less than 183 days a year to pay the government $250 a year.

The pressure on me intensified. There were the traditional detentions during and after street rallies, trials and fines, but this time the police threatened to take away my teenage son because I had been on trial so many times.

At the beginning of 2020, when the Covid-19 epidemic began, journalists started being prosecuted for covering it. When the election campaign began in May, there was further persecution and repression of journalists.

In Belarus, the practice of preventive detentions is often used. Many times before the street protests began there were several police cars parked outside my house. When this happens, I have three options: leave the house and be immediately detained by the police; not leave the house and not get to the demonstration, which I have to cover; or try to run away from the police.

Once, I managed to escape (I had to climb over a fence like a monkey) and took a taxi. Twice, near my house, I was stopped by traffic police and forced to get into a police car, taken to the police station and held for hours until the rallies I was supposed to cover ended.

On election day, policemen were on duty outside my house in the morning, but I did not spend the night at home, so I had the opportunity to cover the election. In late August, when there were mass protests in Gomel against the rigging of the election, I was detained three times near my house and placed in a detention centre.

Several times I was detained in front of my teenage son. Because of this, he was very stressed and six months later he was still feeling the effects of this emotional trauma. My psychological state also deteriorated. I began to feel anxious, I was afraid of detention and arrest and I found it difficult to sleep. Since the election I have a prison bag packed with essential items and books in case of arrest at home.

The police wrote reports that I was allegedly a participant in an unauthorised mass event. Under the law, I can be detained for that but not for practising journalism without accreditation. In court, the reports of participation disappeared and I was instead fined for my journalism.

On February 16, my house was searched as part of a criminal case (not

I have a prison bag packed with essential items in case of arrest

against me). Organised-crime officers searched it for three hours for protest symbols, money, bank cards and other information. As a result, a computer, two cameras, a video camera, hard disks, SD cards and a voice recorder were confiscated.

Working conditions for journalists have changed a lot. Authorities set very high barriers to prevent us obtaining information. That is why we often ask people, activists, to take photos and record audio for us during protests and trials.

There is now a fear – and sometimes terror – in Belarus because of this repression of journalism and civil society. Thousands of people, including journalists, have been forced to leave the country.

Amendments to the law came into force on 1 March, increasing the maximum period of detention for participating in an unauthorised protest from 15 to 30 days and increasing the maximum fine from $350 to $3,000.

These measures have borne fruit and organised street protests have become less common. But the attitude of the people towards the dictator and the police has certainly not changed. It is absolutely negative, full of hatred.

Yauhen Merkis
IS A FREELANCE JOURNALIST, YOUTUBER AND A JOHN SMITH TRUST FELLOW
Being an independent journalist in Belarus has never been easy. Even before the presidential election of 2020 you could get in a lot of trouble just for being a professional journalist and doing your job.

If you want to shoot a video in your hometown, a vox pop for example, the police have the right to detain you for three hours just to check who you are. And even if you have a pass or ID card with you, it won't help you, so it was the easiest way for them to stop you from doing your job.

Alternatively, they can accuse you of working for the independent media ➔

ABOVE: Police detain a protester during the annual Dziady march, November 2020. The march goes from Minsk to a mass grave of Stalin's victims at Kurapaty

→ without accreditation – something that attracts a big fine. And that has happened regularly to a lot of journalists, such as those who work for the independent Belarusian-Polish TV channel Belsat. Since its foundation in 2008, Belsat has tried many times to be registered, but every time it has been refused by the Ministry of Information.

In 2017 after I live-streamed mass protests in Belarusian cities, I had to face the courts three times, and I was fined a total of $1,600.

To try to prevent me from streaming a political rally on 1 May, I was accused of being a hooligan who was cursing in the city centre. The only two witnesses in court were the policemen themselves, and I had to stay in jail for three days. My colleagues ended up covering the protest. Three days is not the maximum detention you can get. In an administrative case, you can be taken to a temporary detention centre for up to 15 days, and this has happened to a lot of journalists.

In more liberal times, this usually happened only when something big took place such as a massive protest or when somebody was too active covering stories the regime didn't want people to hear about. Your house could be searched and your equipment taken away for months while the investigation was ongoing. It has never been easy being a journalist in Belarus.

But 2020 changed everything – for the worse. I have been arrested four times since August and I have been sentenced to a total of 35 days in jail, with the longest term being 27 days. The reason each time was simple: I was accused of participating in forbidden mass street protests. The law has made almost every protest illegal, even though the right to protest and the right for people to

ABOVE: Yauhen Merkis from Belsat has been arrested four times since August 2020

express their thoughts and feelings is written in the constitution.

As proof of my guilt, the court used pictures from CCTV cameras provided by special police units or KGB officers. Although I wore a Press vest and had a Belarusian Association of Journalists ID card, it didn't help.

The conditions in jail were awful. It was cold and damp, the toilet was just a hole in the ground and there was only cold water in the sink. You had the right to shower only once a week.

The authorities decided whether you could receive letters from relatives, friends and colleagues. The food was awful and, after being released, you actually had to pay for all this "comfort" and "security". To prevent your colleagues meeting you on your release, you were driven to the outskirts of town, or even to another town, and released there. Nobody cared

how you would manage to get home. The pressure continues when you're free: surveillance, hacking attacks on your mail and social network accounts, regular visits by police trying to remind you that you don't have the right to do anything "illegal". Every time the doorbell rings, you grab your emergency bag containing the main things you have already packed in case of a possible return to prison.

The law doesn't work in Belarus anymore. Before 2020, the regime tried to at least pretend that the law mattered. Now anything can happen to you. Anytime. Anywhere. It doesn't matter whether you're an activist, a journalist or just a patriot.

Working under such conditions isn't easy and many people have left the country. There are not many independent journalists left. That was always the objective of the police, the Belarus intelligence agency, the KDB, and the regime itself.

But we'll keep fighting for our freedom until we win, even if our weapons are a PC, a video camera or just a pencil. ⊗

50(01):24/26|DOI:10.1177/03064220211012282

> ## You can be taken to a temporary detention centre for up to 15 days, and this has happened to a lot of journalists

Killed by the truth

Lawyer and children's rights campaigner Babar Qadri was shot dead at his house in Kashmir last year. **BILAL AHMAD PANDOW** tells his story

ABOVE: Qadri standing on the chessboard tiles in his garden where he was shot dead

KASHMIRIS ARE KNOWN for being gracious hosts. But last September at Babar Qadri's home, this ritual of hospitality became a prelude to his murder.

Two men went to the human rights lawyer's house, saying they wanted a consultation, and were shown into his garden. Qadri's father, in traditional Kashmiri style, asked for tea to be brought for them. But the guests were not seeking legal advice. They were assassins.

A roaring voice on Indian television and defender of human rights, Qadri was gunned down in his garden in a densely populated area of Hawal in Srinagar, the summer capital of Indian-administered Kashmir.

Immediately after firing upon Qadri, the gunmen fled the area. While lying in the pool of blood, Qadri told his brother Zafar, who is also an advocate, to rush him to the hospital, but he was declared dead on arrival.

Qadri had been at the frontline of civil rights defence for more than a decade and was one of the founder members of Kashmir Thinkers Guild, a local movement for training and mobilising students, civil advocates and environmental rights defenders.

He was also a part of Initiative for Peace and Justice, an organisation seeking to establish peace in the violent region. Qadri organised human rights workshops, awareness drives and non-violent marches to highlight the plight of Kashmiris. He had taken up many lawsuits alleging human rights abuses against children and vigorously advocated for a better criminal justice system for young offenders.

A vocal champion of Kashmir in the media, Qadri's murder was one of the most high-profile killings in the conflict-torn region of Jammu and Kashmir.

His father, Yasin Qadri, told Index that his son was a fearless man.

"He was aware of the threat to his life. However, the police didn't take him seriously," he said.

"Babar time and again raised the alarm and requested security cover, which was never provided to him."

According to Qadri's social media posts he had escaped two previous attacks, but his father said that police thought his son made the threats public for "cheap publicity", saying: "Had the police taken him seriously, it wouldn't have happened."

Qadri was a regular guest on Indian TV, condemning the Indian state for the harsh way it handled Kashmir.

The killers had been waiting for Qadri outside the small lane leading to his home, going into the garden with him and his younger brother.

Qadri told them to wait on the lawn and went inside to tell his mother to prepare some food.

He told her that he would first deal with the clients and then eat.

Little did she know that Qadri would leave this world without even tasting the food she prepared for him.

Qadri stepped out onto a small area tiled like a chessboard – black and yellow – to talk to the men, who were carrying a file with them.

Qadri's father heard raised voices and a few minutes later his parents heard gunshots. The guests had checkmated the kingmaker, as his brother called him, on the chessboard. Tears rolled down her cheeks when Syed Shameema Bano, Qadri's mother, recalled the tragic event. She said: "Babar braved multiple bullets and rushed inside the home. He fell in the corridor with blood oozing out from multiple wounds because of bullets."

Journalist and political analyst Majid Hyderi, a longtime friend of Qadri, told Index that his friend had paid for his bravery with his life. Describing him as "a fearless lion killed in his den".

Hyderi said Qadir had received death threats over the past two years but the Jammu and Kashmir police did nothing, even after he escaped a bid on his life in 2018. →

Even two days before his assassination he tagged police in a tweet about the threat to his life, but police did nothing again

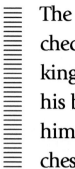

The guests had checkmated the kingmaker – as his brother called him – on the chessboard

→ "Even two days before his assassination he tagged police in a tweet about the threat to his life, but police did nothing again," Hyderi claimed.

"From veteran journalist Syed Shujaat Bukhari [who was gunned down in 2018] to Babar, the police are responsible for having miserably failed to save their lives."

He said Qadri was a vociferous orator and a fearless defender of human rights who loved Kashmir and wanted a peaceful settlement to its problems.

"But apart from all this, he was also a family man – an exemplary father of two daughters," said Hyderi. "I would see him loving and spending lavishly on them. His assassination has killed the home-sweet-home of his daughters as well."

Born on 15 September 1980, Qadri received his early education in Dhobiwan, in the Tangmarg district of Baramulla, and later studied and grew up in Srinagar.

"My son studied in a government school and would outsmart kids of his age from private schools," his father said.

After high school, Qadri took a course in computers for almost a year but information technology didn't hold him for long. He took an entrance exam to the University of Kashmir and was selected for a three-year degree in law, during which time he revived the banned Kashmir University Students Union.

Later, Qadri started practising at the Jammu and Kashmir High Court and challenged the Kashmir High Court Bar Association. The association suspended Babar's membership for "indiscipline", so he formed the Kashmir Lawyers Club.

His father said: "I always used to advise Babar not to challenge the exploiters and the system. He was for an independent Kashmir."

Humayun Qadri told Index that his brother was a kingmaker who never had a lust for power. "He was a democrat in a real sense, not only in his professional acts but in his personal life as well," he said.

Recalling her son's life, Shameema, said that when he had no money to pay for public transport to travel home from school he used to walk. "On return, he never used to complain of not having money. Rather, he used to say that he had a good walk," she recollected.

Qadri married Saima Wani – the daughter of Ghulam Qadir Wani, a philosopher, politician and supporter of Kashmiri independence who was similarly gunned down at his home 22 years ago. Together, they had two daughters, Zahra and Zaineb. Eight-year-old Zahra, the eldest, asked her grandparents: "Why did you offer tea to the killers of my father? Were you fools?"

ABOVE: Babar Qadri's two children, Zahra (left) and Zaineb (right),photographed after his death

Saima Wani told Index that Qadri was a good father. "I couldn't do as much for the kids as he used to," she said, adding that Zahra asked every day about when her father will come back.

"Since the killing of Babar, she has not been able to concentrate on her studies."

Even the burial was not easy for the family, who wanted to go to their family graveyard. After bringing Qadri's body back home from the hospital, there was the worry that the authorities might take it away. "As police and the army cordoned the entire area, in the late evening we took him to our ancestral graveyard at Dhobiwan...for the burial," said Yasin Qadri.

Days before the killing, Qadri posted on social media about the threat to his life, saying: "I urge the state police administration to register an FIR [a report filed by police after they receive notification of a crime] against this [name withheld] who has spread a wrong campaign that I work for agencies. This untrue statement can lead to threats to my life."

According to Qadri's father, two critical incidents could have led to his son's killing.

One is that, on national television, Qadri said "down with India". The other could be the posts Qadri made after the abrogation of Article 370 and 35A of the Indian constitution that provides quasi-autonomy to the region, saying that big corporations would take control of resources in Kashmir.

Laila Qureshi, a family friend, said that Qadri was killed because of the truth. "I don't know anything about his affiliations but all I know is he was speaking the truth and, to my analysis, he was killed because of speaking the truth." She said he had helped her with a legal case. "I found him a generous, good human being [and I] haven't seen many like him. He believed in giving and not taking. He always believed in loving people without any expectations."

Another client, Hina Kazmi, said that Qadri was handling her divorce case. "I remember him many a time going out of

The police investigation

A FORMAL FIR video number 62/2020 under section 302, 7/27 Arms Act and 16/18 UAPA was recorded at the Lal Bazar police station shortly after Qadri's killing, while a special team was set up to investigate the murder on the orders of Vijay Kumar, the inspector general of police for the Kashmir region. However, Qadri's family are on the record as saying that they have no faith in the investigation. After more than five months, three people who had been accused were named by the Qadri family and their domestic help and were sent to prison on remand. Two members of the trio's family vouched for their innocence, claiming they were wrongly implicated and tortured.

ABOVE: Qadri's mother Syed Shameema Bano (right) found him with blood oozing out of bullet wounds

his way to help people without getting anything in return," she said.

Arshid Bashir, a Delhi-based lawyer told Index that Qadri was a fighter by nature. He said: "He was a lively person. He would make his presence felt in the court and was concerned for Kashmir. He used to take cases of stone-pelters [Kashmiri people who throw stones at the police] and the poor pro-bono. He was politically very conscious."

According to Bashir, Qadri believed in electoral politics to address day-to-day issues and would consider democratic institutions the best platform to express one's political opinion.

"He had serious reservations with India and Pakistan alike. He would often speak about their complicity in aggravating the Kashmir issue and bringing it to the present point," he said.

A young university teacher who does not want to be named feels that such killings by unidentified gunmen will have an enormous effect on the psychological health of society in Kashmir. In other words, people, especially those who hold any opinions around Kashmir

politics, will have to be extremely careful what they say. Babar's killing is deeply condemnable. Whatever his political opinions, his voice should not have been silenced. Those who have killed him, and whatever they stand for, do not stand for upholding human rights in Kashmir.

Omar Abdullah, National Conference vice-president and former chief minister of the region, said: "The sense of tragedy is all

the more because he warned of the threat. Sadly, his warning was his last tweet."

People's Conference chairman Sajad Lone tweeted: "One more Kashmiri falls to bullets. Yet another victim of conflict." ✪

Bilal Ahmad Pandow is a researcher and a freelance writer based in Kashmir

50(01):27/29|DOI:10.1177/03064220211012283

Jennings

50(01):30/31|DOI:10.1177/03064220211012284

Our new cartoonist ponders the row over the removal of statues after the global Black Lives Matter campaigns. Statues which honour racist figures, such as slave traders in the UK, the murderous King Leopold II of Belgium and confederate figures in the USA, have been taken down over the past year

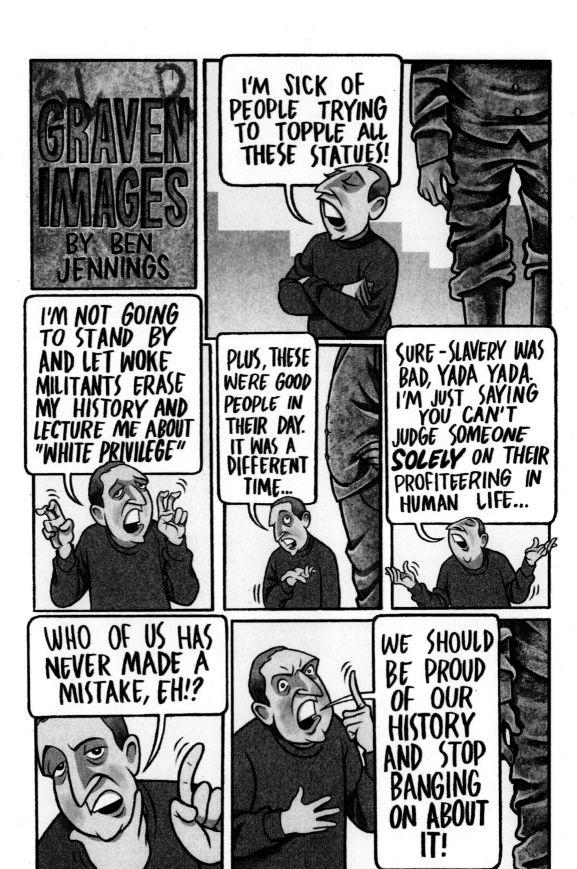

BEN JENNINGS:
an award-winning
cartoonist for The
Guardian and The
Economist whose
work has been
exhibited around the
world

ESSAY

The martial art of free speech

RABBI LAURA JANNER-KLAUSNER and **ARI DELLER** discuss the pitfalls of cancel culture and its effect on free speech

AST YEAR, FOLLOWING complaints, an event at Edinburgh university where Ari studies was relocated off-campus. The event was a session in Krav Maga – an Israeli martial art – taught by an Israeli instructor.

The complaint came from Palestinians on campus who felt that their safety was being threatened. They argued that Krav Maga, which is used by the Israeli Defence Forces and the instructor, who had served in the IDF, could not be separated from their roles in perpetrating Israeli aggression against Palestinians. They said they felt threatened because they had left a violent warzone to study in the UK only to find that what they saw as a threat had followed them. This was a case of campus "cancelling". Both the instructor and the martial art were deemed irredeemably tarnished by their association with the IDF, and so were banned.

Was this cancellation a just one? Under what circumstances should we cancel? When is it right to cast out a person or an institution for views or actions which are deemed unacceptable?

Here is where the difficulty begins. Cancel Culture as a term is ambiguous and broad – covering incidents from Donald Trump's removal from Twitter in January to cessations of friendships between people who differ on whether they would have voted for him in November.

Its use as a "suitcase term", packed with whatever connotations and content might be convenient for those who use it,

ABOVE: Krav Maga lesson in an Israeli paratroopers school, 1955

muddies the waters further.

Especially among those who use it pejoratively, there is inconsistency over its use. Putting al Qaeda on a terror list would never be called "cancellation", but it's not entirely clear why.

Deciding where to draw the line

By relocating the event there was a clear decision: to adopt the narrative of the complainants over that of any prospective defendants.

There isn't necessarily a problem with institutions prioritising one narrative over another, particularly when those institutions espouse democratically elected policies (as student unions do).

But to grant credence to the view of the IDF as a force purely for aggression and evil over, say, a view of the IDF as a morally responsible vehicle for national

protection and liberation is a dangerous one when done without open debate.

And a prerequisite for open debate is that one side of the argument is not cancelled, "no-platformed" or relocated off campus. Cancellations set a dangerous precedent of institutional bias and ignorance when unaccompanied by democratised discourse.

A catch-22 of free speech lies at the heart of understanding Cancel Culture and the difficulty to pin it down.

Fewer regulations on what you can say does not entail free speech.

As the philosopher Caroline West argues, particular kinds of speech (she points to both racist hate speech and pornography) have the effect of silencing other speech. It is easier to see this when thinking about speech as not only communicative but action oriented.

When speech has the ability to intimidate others, or to make them unreceptive to other types of speech, freedom of speech is diminished.

Just look at the squirming victim of a social media "pile-on" to see this in action. It is more appropriate, therefore, to see freedom of speech not as binary but as a continuum, where opposing forces come into tension. We should aim not for an unrealisable total free speech society but for an equilibrium where free speech is maximised. It is with this in mind that we must view Cancel Culture as what it is – a phenomenon involving widespread speech that often has the effect of silencing.

Humanising the abstract

In her video essay on cancel culture, Natalie Wynn (the YouTuber known as ContraPoints) notes its tendency to take an alleged action, presume　➔

> We should aim not for an unrealisable total free speech society but for an equilibrium where free speech is maximised

→ guilt, abstract beyond the details, and identify it integrally with the perpetrator.

Discussing the case of James Charles – a cancelled YouTuber whose downfall was initiated by an accusation that he had tried to trick straight men into thinking they were gay – Wynn notes the predictable string of mutations which result in nuance-removal and abstraction beyond concrete details.

Suddenly the story changes from an initial accusation of a specific action to a presumption of guilt of a vaguer and more deep-set crime – that of being a morally detestable person.

"James Charles is accused of trying to trick straight men" becomes "James Charles tried to trick straight men" and then "James Charles is sexually manipulative". Such a move makes defending oneself against accusations all the more difficult. Repudiating a claim that a particular action was taken involves providing evidence that the action could not have, or is unlikely to have, been taken. But it's less clear what criteria would have to be fulfilled in order to successfully defend oneself against having a particular character trait.

This makes it all the easier to be cast out, particularly from the online community. Such a fundamental attack on a person makes them infectious by association – untouchable.

Consider the conditions which exacerbate the move from allegations that an action took place to the unquestioning

Such a fundamental attack on a person makes them infectious by association - untouchable

tarnishing of a person. The incentives that social media creates for quick of compelling messages drives shocking character assassinations. Cancel Culture's labelling can be seen as symptomatic of an era where people present themselves using a few carefully chosen words, and choose their allies and enemies based on the same.

In other words, it's a necessity of online interaction with billions of users that one makes snap judgments about others in relation to oneself. Amidst the haze of a galaxy of online profiles it is simply easier to think: "James Charles: sexually manipulative". To humanise, however, is to resist this urge to essentialise a person with one or two adjectives. It is to view people and their actions holistically, to understand the layers in their personalities and the nuances of their actions.

To humanise is also to leave room for rehabilitation, not just retribution. Cancel Culture can be profoundly unforgiving. It can take earnest missteps, or questions of clarification made in good faith, and punish them with full force, deterring others from stepping out of line and penalising perpetrators beyond the scope of their transgressions. It can deprive people of a second, or sometimes a first, chance.

So, given Cancel Culture's disposition to dehumanise, when is it appropriate to cancel? One such occasion is when our interlocutors have themselves taken the step of disrespecting our humanity.

Jean-Paul Sartre writes in Anti-Semite and Jew: "Never believe that anti-Semites are completely unaware of the absurdity of their replies. They know their remarks are frivolous, open to challenge. But they are amusing themselves, for it is their adversary who is obliged to use words responsibly, since he believes in words...

"They delight in acting in bad faith, since they seek not to persuade by sound argument but to intimidate and disconcert... his conviction is strong because he has chosen first of all to be impervious."

It is easy to relate to engaging with

ABOVE: Jean-Paul Sartre in Venice, 1967

people such as this, whose discourse is tedious and futile precisely because they do not respect their conversational counterparts. It is the words of these people which often diminish free speech. They suck the oxygen from debating halls and leave soot-smirched frustration in their trails.

Cancel Culture, then, is a movement which threatens to push on in a social media-driven offensive against understanding others with compassion. It co-conspires with fast labelling to dismiss others and often diminish healthy discourse.

It should be met with an emphasis on empathy and human understanding. However, as West has argued, engagement with all speech does not make for free speech.

We should be wary of the pitfalls of cancellation while implementing responsibility in choosing to disengage from bad-faith actors who themselves dehumanise. ⊗

Rabbi Laura Janner-Klausner is a leadership consultant and the former Senior Rabbi to Reform Judaism. Ari Deller is a writer and philosophy undergraduate at the University of Edinburgh

50(01):32/34|DOI:10.1177/03064220211012285

SPECIAL REPORT

The truth is, everyone in China is a hostage. Some may be wealthier than others, some more aware than others of the prison bars that surround them, but everyone is spiritually incarcerated by the Chinese Communist Party

MA JIAN ON 100 YEARS OF THE CHINESE COMMUNIST PARTY | THE HUMAN FACE AND THE BOOT P54

Burning through censorship

MARK FRARY and **MARTIN BRIGHT** talk to one of the
founders of GreatFire, an anti-firewall collective which for
10 years has been unblocking news for people in China

ABOVE: The Great Wall of China

A S THE CHINESE Communist Party celebrates its 100th birthday, a shifting, shapeless organisation that is one of its antagonists celebrates its 10th.

In 2011, GreatFire launched its first project to "help bring transparency to online censorship in China".

Since then, its GreatFire Analyser tool has accumulated a vast amount of data on the blocking of websites and keywords by China's Great Firewall. The tool has recently been renamed as Blocky.

In the past decade, the scope of its work has expanded and is now focused on helping Chinese people freely to access

The people behind Great Wall are largely anonymous, both to the outside world but also to each other – it's safer that way

information through a range of projects.

The project was co-founded by a trio using the pseudonyms Charlie Smith, Percy Alpha and Martin Johnson.

"The people behind GreatFire are largely anonymous to the outside world and also to each other – it's safer that way," said Smith in a recent call with Index.

"I know that we are all very, very closely tied to China and have been for a long time. What I can say is that we're not anti-China – although there are certain things we don't love."

He said that in the beginning, GreatFire was designed to educate people that ➜

→ things were being blocked – and not by only the country's Great Firewall. There is also the domestic censorship of local social media platforms.

"The censorship that takes place on those platforms is very advanced, very technologically savvy," he said. "The Chinese authorities put the burden of censorship onto these companies and these companies are worth billions of dollars, so they need to take that censorship seriously."

As a result, the organisation set up its own, uncensored versions of the platforms. Its FreeWeChat platform restores and republishes censored information from WeChat, China's ubiquitous and most popular application.

FreeWeibo is an "unsanitised" version of the popular Chinese social media network Weibo, with more than 300,000 censored and deleted posts restored.

The group also provides a censorship circumvention tool called Free Browser which it offers to human rights and freedom of expression organisations without charge. It has been used by more than 1,000 people.

Chinese internet users looking for censored news stories about government

From green to red

GreatFire's Blocky tool uses traffic light colour-coding to track increasing censorship of British and US news websites. The frequency with which access to the BBC's worldwide site has been blocked along with other sites such as The Guardian and The New York Times has been steadily growing in the last eight years. These sites were blocked or content censored most days in 2021.

corruption, politics, scandals and other "sensitive" information can find them through the FreeBrowser StartPage project – and more than 13 million have done so.

In recent years, GreatFire has started focusing its attention on Western companies operating in China, and on Apple in particular.

"Apple is very much involved in helping the Chinese authorities with their censorship efforts so we launched a website called Apple Censorship, where we basically monitor what Apple is censoring in different App Stores around the world and we put pressure on Apple to basically stop," said Smith.

Apple is particularly well placed to censor because it controls the App Store, which is often the only way to get an app on one of its phones. This is something that the UK government, in the shape of the Competition and Markets Authority (CMA), has started to take an interest in.

"The thing with Apple is they set the tone for a lot of other companies because they say one thing and then they act in a different way," said Smith. "In the rest of the world, Apple positions itself as being this great advocate for privacy and for freedom of expression, and that Apple iPhone is the tool that helps to enable that connection – but in China that is totally not the case.

"If you buy an iPhone, you're basically submitting to the censorship apparatus. You have no way of getting around that censorship with an Apple device."

Apple did not respond to Index's request for comment. However, the company has published a policy outlining its commitment to human rights.

In it, it says: "As a global technology company we feel a deep sense of responsibility to make technology for people that respects their human rights, empowers them with useful tools and information, and enhances their overall quality of life. We do that with our uncompromising commitment to security and user privacy – setting the industry standard for minimising personal data collection. We build privacy protections

into everything we make – from products like iPhone, to services like Apple Pay, to our comprehensive review process for every app on the App Store.

"Hand in hand with the privacy of our users is our commitment to freedom of information and expression. Our products help our customers communicate, learn, express their creativity and exercise their ingenuity. We believe in the critical importance of an open society in which information flows freely, and we're convinced the best way we can continue to promote openness is to remain engaged, even where we may disagree with a country's laws."

But Apple is not alone in getting criticism from Smith. He says that other companies like Microsoft have been in China for a long time. Social media sites such as Facebook and Twitter are not officially in China, but they carry a lot of ads paid for by the Chinese state and Chinese companies.

"What we're worried about is that other foreign companies say it's better to be in the China market, even if it means that [they] have to – and I'm putting this in air quotes – 'adhere to local laws'."

The organisation is keeping close tabs on Hong Kong, in the wake of the introduction of the national security law.

"As of today, Hongkongers have the same internet freedom or media freedom as the UK does," said Smith. "They can access every website that you can, they can use any VPN that you can, they can use the privacy applications you can. So, at the moment, we don't see that there's been one instance of a website being blocked by an internet service provider."

But Apple's popularity in Hong Kong means it could come under pressure.

"In Hong Kong, Apple's penetration is huge – every other phone is an iPhone. They have enormous power and control," said Smith.

"If the Chinese government tells them that Hong Kong is under their control, then [Apple] could get rid of all of these VPN apps and all these privacy apps. They could wreak a lot of havoc.

"There was a story recently about Facebook censoring information related to Hong Kong on their platform…I don't think that that is widespread. So, at the moment Hong Kong is pretty much just like any other country, but that could change at any time."

Although it will not affect Apple's vice-like grip on apps for iPhone users, GreatFire has recently launched an anti-censorship App Maker allowing anybody to create their own app aimed at smartphones run on the Android operating system and to download apps from anywhere, not just from a centrally controlled store.

"Our App Maker project allows you to create an app that has this anti-censorship technology built into it," said Smith. "Once you've created that you can share it with your followers or upload

We started GreatFire before Xi Jinping took power. Before then, there was great hope

The Great Firewall

China's first brush with the internet came in the late 1980s through links between scientific academic institutions.

On 20 September 1987, Professor Qian Tianbai of the Beijing Municipal Computer Application Research Institute sent the country's first email with the subject Crossing the Great Wall to Join the World.

It took until 20 April 1994 for the country to be officially connected to the internet when a Chinese network of education and scientific research organisations joined it through the USA's Sprint Corporation.

Controls followed just three years later when the ministry of public security introduced rules that prohibited individuals from using the internet to "harm national security, disclose state secrets or injure the interests of the state or society" or for actions which incited resistance to China's constitution, sought to overthrow the government or socialist system, undermined national unification, distorted the truth, spread rumours, destroyed social order, provided sexually suggestive material or encouraged gambling, violence or murder.

A wide range of technologies have since been deployed: banning the ranges of the IP addresses that direct users to websites, using deep packet inspection to identify the users of VPNs, and keyword-based filtering and search redirection.

This combination of technologies is known as the Great Firewall with the Golden Shield Project, launched in 2003 using technology from the likes of Cisco, at the heart of it. Tens of thousands of workers have taken part in building the "wall".

It now routinely censors websites affiliated to banned organisations such as the religious organisation Falun Gong, news sources that talk about banned subjects such as the Tiananmen Square massacre and Taiwan, pornographic sites and other websites considered to be subversive.

it to Google Play but also in alternative Android app stores as well. You can make the download link available directly to people or make a QR code.

"Creating the anti-censorship technology is actually not the hard part. The hard part is the distribution, which is the same for any app. How do you get into the hands of users?"

The organisation has started offering its anti-censorship technology to the more than 50 million developers around the world who use GitHub to find and share code for their projects.

"We've made a code base that runs that anti-censorship technology, open source and available freely," said Smith.

It is not just the stereotypical spotty coders in their bedrooms who can use this freely available code.

"Facebook could integrate that code into their Android app," he said. "If people were downloading it in China, Facebook would work. So even if the government decided it was going to cut off Facebook in Hong Kong, it would still

work. "That can be an important thing because things like Facebook are used for organising and sharing information. We want those bigger organisations to adopt this technology as well."

Why do Smith and his co-founders do this? "We started GreatFire before [Chinese president] Xi Jinping took power," said Smith. "Before then, there was great hope. Yes, a great hope that China would be, you know, a member of the global community in good standing. China would be an active participant for good in the world. And I don't think anyone predicted what actually happened.

"It's become a lot more difficult. To tell you the truth I don't know how many of us would have committed to this project if we were starting today in this environment." ⊗

Mark Frary is an associate editor at Index and Martin Bright is the editor of Index

50(01):36/39|DOI:10.1177/03064220211012294

'Extremely important and profoundly disturbing'
ARCHBISHOP DESMOND TUTU

'A withering assault on the murderous Rwandan regime of Paul Kagame – very driven, very impassioned'
JOHN LE CARRÉ

'An extremely important and profoundly disturbing book'
ARCHBISHOP DESMOND TUTU

Do Not Disturb

The Story of a Political Murder and an African Regime Gone Bad

MICHELA WRONG

'A withering assault on the murderous regime of Kagame, and a melancholy love song to the last dreams of the African Great Lakes'
JOHN LE CARRÉ

The party is your idol

TIANYU M FANG looks at how the Chinese state is adapting its methods of control to the 21st century and how young people are resisting

N THE SUMMER of 1921, Marxists from all over China gathered secretly in a house in Shanghai's French Concession, as their countrymen struggled in seemingly unending political turmoil. Among the representatives was Mao Zedong, from Changsha, who would eventually take power in 1949.

The Shanghai meeting was one of the most significant historical events in modern Chinese history – the founding of the Chinese Communist Party (CCP).

A century later, after a world war, a civil war and countless turbulent revolutions, the same house that once hosted China's Marxist revolutionaries now finds itself surrounded by Japanese cocktail bars, high-end European restaurants, a Lululemon and, most recently, a Shake Shack. The neighbourhood is now known as Xintiandi, a favourite hang-out for Shanghai's young internet celebrities. The house itself has become a communist museum. While tourists frequent it during the day, few shoppers and drinkers notice the old French house as night draws in.

To most Chinese young people today, life is no longer about communal life and political dogma. They feel less attachment to the party which used to arrange jobs, education and housing for their parents and grandparents. Becoming a member often means an easier career in public service or state-owned enterprises, but fewer are willing to join.

Forget about Mao's long-winded writings – the majority of China's Gen Z has never lived through the abject poverty that the CCP claims to have lifted China out of. Nor do they have lived experience of the Great Leap Forward, the Cultural Revolution or the 1989 protests. Like young people elsewhere, those born in the 1990s and 2000s now spend their spare time watching viral short videos, following Korean pop stars on social media and spending disposable income on both domestic and foreign-branded products via e-commerce apps.

In the era of traditional media, the party could control newspapers and broadcasters. To exert power in a digital world is much more difficult when information channels – social media apps, news aggregators and content producers – are no longer fully owned by the state.

Despite this, the party is fighting back. It has not always succeeded: In 2019, the CCP launched Xuexi Qiangguo, a smartphone app that aggregates news articles, videos and quizzes about CCP ideology, government policy and President Xi Jinping's newest directives. While it quickly climbed up the ranks on Chinese app stores, it was only because party cadres were required to download it.

Everyone knows it is old-fashioned propaganda, and it has little appeal to Chinese young people. A young government employee in southern China whom I met was finishing his Xuexi Qiangguo quizzes – only because he had to – before going on a long rant about Xi's personal cult. There are online tutorials and cheat tools that allow users to get higher scores without actually learning the material.

The CCP knows that to increase its appeal to China's consumerist, digital-native generation of citizens, it has to adapt more skilfully to the internet and social media to recentralise its power in the information space. Bringing Marxism online is just not going to do the trick.

When Bilibili was founded a decade ago in Shanghai, it was a niche video-sharing platform popular among China's anime lovers, webcasting Japanese television series with Chinese subtitles at a time of fraught relations between the two countries.

Today, the Nasdaq-listed company is the preferred video site among Chinese young people, with approximately 200 million monthly active users. Its content ranges from parody clips of Donald Trump to Khan Academy-style chemistry lectures. It offers the popular feature of *danmaku*, which allows users to post comments that float over the video, adding an interactive component to the viewing experience.

Bilibili is uniquely positioned for content producers to reach young Chinese audiences, which might explain why the platform's favourite uploader, as measured by the total number of likes, is the Communist Youth League, a branch of the CCP responsible for mobilising young people.

The Communist Youth League has 7.75 million followers, and its most-viewed videos include a compilation of "violence and chaos" in the 2019 Hong Kong protests and clips of officials boasting about China's military capabilities.   →

Its content ranges from parody clips of Donald Trump to Khan Academy-style chemistry lectures

→ Jasmin Zheng, a university student from Beijing, used to go to Bilibili for a Japanese television series but she has sensed the platform's transformation. "I can feel the obvious political propaganda," Zheng told Index, adding that she always saw patriotic videos on the homepage despite having never followed any relevant accounts.

"The [state-affiliated] outlets like to publish videos that contrast China with foreign countries to show the superiority of Chinese society, and the comments are often overwhelmingly supportive of these narratives," Zheng added.

One other popular account is Guan Video, a multimedia studio with more than three million followers. Although it is a private company, Guan produces

> Like young people elsewhere, those born in the 1990s and 2000s now spend their spare time watching viral short videos, following Korean pop stars on social media and spending disposable income on both domestic and foreign-branded products via e-commerce apps

video content for Hu Xijin, editor-in-chief of the Global Times, a state-owned, bilingual tabloid known for its sensational reporting and nationalist editorials. The studio also publishes content featuring other prominent political commentators, including Zhang Weiwei, the Fudan University professor who advocates the "China model" and hosts the popular patriotic television show China Now.

Bilibili is not the only Chinese online platform for political mobilisation. The Communist Youth League has garnered more than 15 million followers on Weibo, the Chinese equivalent of Twitter, by posting (or, more accurately, mostly reposting) viral video clips, memes and sometimes rap music featuring strong nationalist tones.

Shaohua Guo, associate professor of Chinese at Carleton College, in Minnesota, USA, has found in a study that state-sponsored social media campaigns have involved a transition from the notorious Maoist formalities and rituals to language that caters to popular audiences.

Guo's paper shows that the Communist Youth League appropriates elements of Chinese fan culture to amass a young supporter base, arousing nationalistic sentiments in an approachable fashion. The party-state is no longer a political machine but an idol often known as Brother China (a-zhong gege) to its fans.

"This is the logic of online media," said Guo, whose recent book is The Evolution of the Chinese Internet: Creative Visibility in the Digital Public. "It's very important to get the attention of users. If you want to gain popularity, you'll have to change the way you talk to the audience."

The party has also adopted tactics to shape public opinion using social media marketing strategies. Stanford scholars Jennifer Pan and Yingdan Lu found that Chinese government accounts often used clickbait to obtain more views and likes, reaching a greater audience in ways similar to commercial and celebrity accounts.

Another study showed that the state fabricated social media posts to shape public opinion using sock-puppet accounts, distracting users from sensitive discussions.

When Tzuyu, a Taiwanese singer based in South Korea, waved the Republic of China flag after the democratic election of Tsai Ing-wen in Taiwan, young Chinese nationalists bombarded Taiwanese political pages on Facebook with internet memes. Similar campaigns emerged during the Hong Kong protests in 2019. While these movements

ABOVE: Cosplayers dressed as mascots of Bilibili, a Chinese video-sharing website. The Communist Youth League is one of its most prolific uploaders

started as grassroot actions, state media accounts, including the official newspaper People's Daily, praised their patriotism. (China's Great Firewall prevents users from accessing certain foreign websites, including Facebook and Twitter, but there are ways to bypass it – especially when the state offers tacit approval.)

China's growing consumerism, too, has become useful political leverage. As Daryl Morey, then manager of the NBA team Houston Rockets, voiced support for Hong Kong's protesters on Twitter, young Chinese on social media called for boycotts against the NBA, and broadcasters stopped airing the basketball games despite the NBA's immense popularity in China.

Foreign companies have come under fire for including Taiwan and Hong Kong as countries in dropdown lists on their websites. Designer houses Versace, Coach and Givenchy were boycotted because they printed shirts that listed Hong Kong, Macau and Taiwan without adding the word "China". Celebrities embraced in China are not immune to political scrutiny, either. South Korean boy band BTS angered Chinese fans after accepting an award that commemorated South Korean-USA relations – a move that invoked the memory of China's involvement in the Korean War. "Nation before idols" became a popular trope on Chinese social media as a way of fans   →

→ showing their loyalty to the country.

There's the internet, and there's the Chinese internet. While Beijing exploits social media for propaganda, it continues to reinforce its control of the internet through blocking and censorship.

The blocking of foreign platforms allows the rise of domestic ones more tailored to the Chinese audience and compliant with the state's requests.

Censorship alone does not mean that citizens do not get to express their discontent with government actions. Academics have found that China's censorship regime is most concerned about information that may lead to collective actions, and most posts critical of the government are left intact on the Chinese internet. But once the censor judges that a discussion could jeopardise social stability,

because there was not enough data.

While the government controls major media publications, social media platforms have enabled the rise of "self-media" – accounts operated by individuals or private companies that provide social commentaries or news content on WeChat or Weibo.

Although some of these accounts have become hubs of misinformation, they often provide platforms for citizen journalists and commentators whose viewpoints are unavailable in state-owned media due to political sensitivities.

Beijing has recently issued a directive that prohibits private accounts from publishing content related to current affairs without a government-issued news permit, effectively banning most individual publishers. The decision

way that China does. While it remains unclear whether this will become the new international norm, increased state regulation of the internet is ever more appealing to governments worldwide. In addition to efforts by Iranian and Russian governments to replicate China's Great Firewall, the blocking of Chinese apps by the USA and India could similarly contribute to this trend.

Suji Yan, a Chinese software engineer, entrepreneur and labour rights advocate, is more optimistic. His team has built software that allows users to post encrypted information on social media platforms, allowing users to protect their privacy and freedom from censorship. "Censorship is part of the cyber leviathan created by the government and agencies using manpower, technology and money," he said.

"Cryptography – whether it is encrypted information or cryptocurrency or the broader crypto network – is one approach to allow users to regain the right to privacy and self-defence in a networked society."

Propaganda in the age of social media also means there are now more actors involved. As the Communist Youth League's popularity on Bilibili shows, the government isn't the only player in shaping China's internet landscape – media institutions, privately-owned tech firms, cultures, subcultures and a growing number of internet users all contribute to an ever more complex network of forces shaping narratives and discourses.

> A former programmer at Bytedance, which owns the popular video app TikTok, was asked to develop an algorithm that cuts off livestreams in Uighur

that liberty is put to an end.

"Social media companies usually have a department that is responsible for censorship," Jiajun Zeng, a former product manager in China, told Index. One internet company he used to work for maintains a team of more than 10,000 content moderators.

Self-censorship by platforms is becoming smarter and less labour-intensive with natural language-processing algorithms and keyword filtering. A former programmer at Bytedance, which owns the popular video app TikTok, was asked to develop an algorithm that cuts off livestreams in Uighur on its Chinese platform, because moderators did not speak the language and did not want to be penalised by regulators. He did not eventually do it

followed the arrest of Zhang Zhan, a Chinese citizen who wrote critically about the country's early response to the coronavirus. Zhang was sentenced to four years in prison.

As the CCP reaches its centenary this year, expect to see public displays of celebration – ceremonies and documentaries on television and propaganda banners in the streets. In Shaanxi province, home to Mao Zedong's old revolutionary base of Yan'an, tour guides say they are prepared for a surge in visitors this year as domestic travel returns to normal. Most celebrations, however, will happen on social media platforms.

The CCP under Xi has been promoting the idea of "cyber sovereignty", maintaining that governments have the right to regulate their internet the

"Sometimes these players are in a co-operative relationship," said Guo, who rejects the binary view that the internet is either a force of liberalisation or a tool for autocratic control. "But sometimes they are in a competitive relationship. At other times, they can be in an adversarial relationship." ⊗

Tianyu M Fang is a writer and journalist. He covers Chinese politics, technology, and culture

50(01):41/44|DOI:10.1177/03064220211012299

FOR EVERYONE WHO WANTS TO UNDERSTAND 'CANCEL CULTURE'

Cynical ~~CRITICAL~~ THEORIES

How Universities Made Everything about Race, Gender, and Identity – and Why This Harms Everybody

HELEN PLUCKROSE AND JAMES LINDSAY

BOOK OF THE YEAR

The Times | Sunday Times | Financial Times

'Brilliant' *Daily Telegraph*

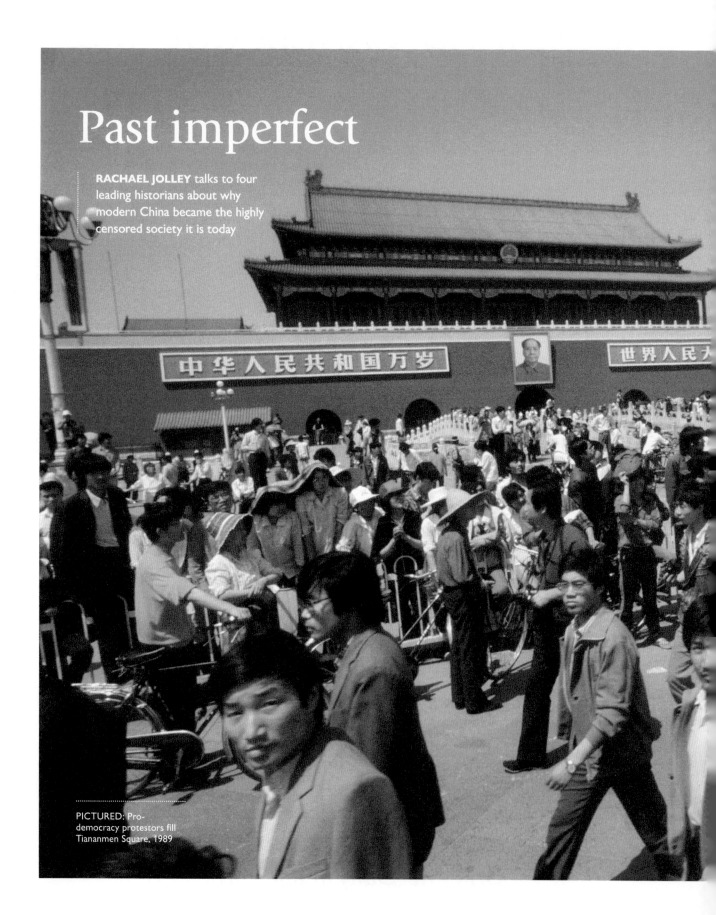

Past imperfect

RACHAEL JOLLEY talks to four leading historians about why modern China became the highly censored society it is today

PICTURED: Pro-democracy protestors fill Tiananmen Square, 1989

CHINESE GOVERNMENT ATTEMPTS to censor doctors who wanted to alert the world to a new Covid virus in January 2020 are a recent example of a society in which citizens are penalised for saying anything that might show China in a negative light.

For those who study the country's past, this attitude is not leftfield but draws on decades of government decision-making. Index spoke to historians about whether there were moments during the 20th and 21st centuries that pushed China's governments towards greater censorship.

Timothy Cheek, professor and director of the Institute of Asian Research at the University of British Columbia, highlighted three figures who have had huge influence on China's embrace of censorship. These are Sun Yat-sen in the 1920s, Mao Zedong in the 1940s and Xi Jinping – the current president – today.

Sun Yat-sen, often called the father of modern-day China, signed the Sun-Joffe agreement in 1923. Cheek said: "He made the deal with the Soviets because nobody else would fund him. And he believed in one party, one ideology, one voice, one leader, and it was him. And he justified that dictatorship by saying the Chinese people were not ready for democracy."

Cheek said that to understand China's attitude towards freedom of expression and censorship it is essential ➔

Even elites and governments need to have a story to tell themselves to make their bureaucrats and their people feel good

ABOVE: Japanese troops climb up the harbour wall in Shanghai during the Sino-Japanese War in 1937

→ to understand "thought reform". He said: "As far as the party leadership is concerned, it's a good thing. It's like Bible study.

"Even elites and governments need to have a story to tell themselves to make their bureaucrats and their people feel good."

For China's leaders, it is about telling China's story well "to themselves as well as to the world". He added: "Mao's big contribution was that propaganda is not just for them."

Sei Jeong Chin, professor in international studies at Ewha Woman's University in Seoul, South Korea, pointed to the Japanese invasion of Chinese territory from 1931 and the Sino-Japanese war as incredibly significant in

making it easier for the post-World War II Chinese Communist Party to establish strict control of the media in the 1950s.

Before the war with Japan, independent newspapers still flourished in China. "Thus, if Japan did not encroach upon Chinese territory from 1931 and did not wage war against China, I think the trajectory of the media history could have gone quite differently," she said.

"The confiscation of privately-owned commercial newspapers by the Japanese military in the Japanese-occupied areas during wartime had significant impact on

the nationalisation of media in the early People's Republic of China."

There was also censorship of the media in China by the nationalist government during World War II which made it, said Chin, easier for the CCP to nationalise the media in the early 1950s.

Rana Mitter, professor of the history and politics of modern China at Oxford University, said constant war in the 20th century was a factor in creating a locked-down society. "Whether it's civil war – which, of course, is very, very common – whether it's the warlord battles of the

A factor in the government's response was the fear of what was happening with the fall of other communist regimes, including the Soviet Union

ABOVE: A poster of Sun Yat-sen, 1927, between two nationalist flags. The words read 'the revolution is not yet completed; your comrades must continue to make efforts'. Chiang Kai-shek is shown below

1920s, whether it was the actual Civil War of 1946 to 1949, or whether it was the Cultural Revolution – which you could regard actually as a form of civil war as well – the point is that all of these very, very violent, destructive events polarised politics in a way that was intended to reduce the space for more liberal belief in debate, and uncensored alternatives became much narrower."

He added: "China, of course, is not in a literal sense at war today, but if you turn on the television in China, you'll see there's a great deal of militarisation of society.

"The People's Liberation Army is certainly brought up frequently as an exemplar for society. And in some ways that echoes earlier eras in China's history when that was also true. You also see that war metaphors and analogies have been used very extensively, including, of course, during the Covid crisis."

A sense that certain discussions should just not be had at all harks back to Confucianism, said Mitter, and results in a societal self-censorship.

There are, and were, places and ways to get around restrictions.

Both Cheek and Mitter point to colonial enclaves in cities such as Shanghai in the 1920s being used as ways of escaping controls and publishing things that were illegal in the rest of the country. This also happened in reverse.

Jeffrey Wasserstrom, a chancellor's professor in history at the University of California, Irvine, said: "If they wanted to attack foreigners, they would go to the Chinese-controlled places and publish things there.

"This resonates a lot right now with people in Hong Kong [who have] to go abroad in order to keep saying the kinds of things that they used to be able to say there."

People in China are allowed freedom in only some aspects of their lives, Wasserstrom added. "You get choices at the supermarket, choices at the cinema, but you don't get the choices at the ballot box." But because they do have some choices, many citizens feel it is a more open society, with more options, than it was a few decades ago.

There are elements of control and surveillance that the government has been able to "sell" to its citizens as a public good, and this is not always understood by the rest of the world. Mitter said: "They've managed to create a narrative in which state control of all this data is, for many people, not terrifying but reassuring."

Wasserstrom added that another element of control was the way that the PRC was "saturating people with what Xi

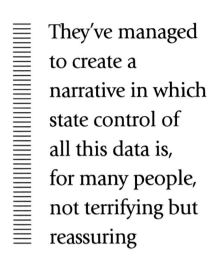

They've managed to create a narrative in which state control of all this data is, for many people, not terrifying but reassuring

calls 'the good China story' – the story the way he wants you to look at the world".

He cites 1989 and Tiananmen Square as being historically significant for adding more control. In the years leading up to then, China's government had loosened its grip somewhat, but in 1989 big protests spread across the country. A factor in the government's response was the fear of what was happening with the fall of other communist regimes, including the Soviet Union.

"I think that shaped the censorship →

战无不胜的马克思列宁主义、毛泽东思想万岁!

ABOVE: A 1967 propaganda poster featuring Mao, Stalin, Lenin, Engels and Marx

→ to try to be particularly restrictive on anything that had the possibility to connect people across social and geographical borders," he said.

Looking back, do the historians see moments when the world could have reacted differently to China, smoothing the way to greater openness?

What would have made some difference, according to Mitter, was deeper knowledge. "There was an underinvestment of time and effort in understanding what made China distinctive and what its historical conditions were," he said. "That is an opportunity that we have missed and have continued to miss, actually."

Wasserstrom feels there were moments when the Chinese government really wanted a position or role internationally, and those were the times when change was

China may not be democratic, but sure as sugar it's globalised, and I don't think most Chinese are going to buy this level of control in the future

possible: "There could have been more of a pushback at the time of the Olympics."

Western figures also need to be careful not to normalise Chinese censorship, said Wasserstrom, referring to a speech by Apple CEO Tim Cook which appeared to reinforce the Chinese government's control of the internet.

Cheek's thoughts on missed opportunities and the possibilities in the future are mixed. "We can't change China, but we can nudge China," he said.

Chin is less than optimistic: "Nationalistic 'netizens' as regime defenders often play a role of

delegitimising dissenting voices in online spaces. Thus, it is still unclear whether the internet and social media can function as a force for political liberalisation."

But Cheek feels that Chinese people will not be happy with this level of control in the future. "China may not be democratic, but sure as sugar it's globalised, and I don't think most Chinese are going to buy this." ⊗

Rachael Jolley is a contributing editor to Index on Censorship

50(01):46/50|DOI:10.1177/03064220211012301

BELOW: Two customers in a supermarket in the Chinese city of Huaibei

Turkey changes its tune

The government in Ankara used to crack down on Maoists, but as Turkey has become part of the Modern Silk Road, **KAYA GENÇ** finds that the new alliance with China means the thousands of Uighurs living in exile present a huge political challenge

N JANUARY, WHEN hundreds of young Turks defied the authorities to protest against the appointment of a pro-government rector at Boğaziçi, Turkey's most prestigious college, Istanbul's governor quickly imposed a blanket ban on all marches

This ban also extended to a group of Uighurs standing silently outside Istanbul's Chinese embassy carrying case details of their relatives. Around a dozen women wearing face masks and headscarves, and indistinguishable from pious Turks, had been demanding the release of their loved ones from Chinese detention. During previous weeks, police had arrested numerous Uighur men, saying they were members of Isis.

Unlike the students, who banged pans, sang and carried rainbow banners,

these protesters said little, but stood their ground.

For the Turkish government, accustomed to branding its critics as degenerates fighting the will of Muslims, the Uighur protests present an awkward picture and a potential political challenge. Religiously Muslim and ethnically Turkish, the Uighurs and their treatment by China should have been a propaganda opportunity for the ruling AKP.

In Xinjiang, authorities reportedly have held up to 1.8 million Uighurs and other Muslim minorities in internment camps since 2017. Turkish president Recep Tayyip Erdoğan talked of the "genocide" of China's Uighurs back in 2009, when he fashioned himself as a conservative democrat in Western capitals. Twelve years later, Turkey's closest allies are Russia,

ABOVE: A supporter of China's Muslim Uighur minority wears a face mask with the flag of East Turkestan in Istanbul

China and Iran, and the governing AKP is muted about Xinjiang.

Around 50,000 Uighur people live in Turkey. It was in August last year that around 100 of them began the regular protests outside the embassy. They demanded the Chinese government account for the whereabouts of their missing family members. A 2017 extradition bill signed between Turkey and China led to fears they might lose their Turkish sanctuary. Finally on 13 January, after Istanbul's governor intervened, the Chinese consulate accepted enquiries about the fate ➜

Religiously Muslim and ethnically Turkish, the Uighurs and their treatment by China should have been a propaganda opportunity for the Turkish government

→ of their relatives. The episode was symptomatic of the checkered relationship between Turkey and China.

After the communist state was founded in 1949, Turkey didn't recognise the People's Republic of China. For 22 years the NATO member kept its distance from the Maoist Beijing. Ankara pursued a Pan-Turkism foreign policy, rooting for the independence of former Soviet states Kazakhstan and Turkmenistan and welcoming the fall of the Berlin Wall and the disintegration of the Soviet Union. Deeply conservative, Turkey has battled Marxists since its foundation in 1923, choosing to align with the capitalist West instead: red radicals garnered little sympathy in the former seat of the Islamic Caliphate.

Turkey's axis shifted after Ahmet Davutoğlu, an international relations professor intent on a Neo-Ottoman future became Turkey's foreign minister in 2009.

Under his command, Turkey's foreign ministry put forging better ties with neighbours ahead of serving as Nato's eastern-border security guard.

As Ankara made its Eurasian love known in Washington and Brussels, commerce between China and Turkey snowballed from $238 million in 1990 to $24 billion in 2012, the year China's newly-elected leader, Xi Jinping, visited Turkey.

New projects, including nuclear energy schemes and a Chinese-built 5,000km railway, were announced. Over the last decade the Modern Silk Road project, connecting China with Caucasian and Central Asian countries, has defined Turkish perceptions of China.

"Turkey is trying to appease Beijing in order to continue securing loans from China for its major construction projects," said Soner Çağaptay, who runs the Washington Institute for Near East Policy's Turkish research programme.

"Hot money in Istanbul's stockmarket is drying up. Turkey's growth model is based on mega construction projects, and Chinese sub-prime loans are a crucial part of that. Chinese money drives investment and demand in Turkey, helping create jobs, metro stations, new bridges and highways. For the government, China is a country that can provide Turkey with a lifeline should Turkey's economy collapse. To this end, Ankara started a 'charm offensive' toward the Chinese."

Çağaptay puts charm offensive in inverted commas because "it doesn't involve being nice to the Chinese. It's about being 'not un-nice' to them. This means preventing a harsh critique of China's Uighur policies".

Turkey's present-day courting of China has a rationale, but it still rattles many. Those who once adored Beijing feel particularly uneasy. Ragıp Duran, a 60-year-old veteran reporter, was a Maoist in his youth. Showing sympathy for the Chinese regime was sufficient reason then for Turkish police to detain and torture young intellectuals.

Duran followed with interest stories on the Chinese communist experiment, working on Aydınlık, a magazine sympathetic to Mao Zedong's thinking.

At that time, Turkey considered Duran and his circle to be enemies of the state.

"In the 1970s they didn't make distinctions between Trotskyism, Maoism and other sects. We were all communists Turkey was set on destroying."

Once he learned of the extremities of the Cultural Revolution, Duran changed course. "In our circles we viewed the Cultural Revolution as a positive thing because this was the official party-line. Then I learned that works by the Turkish poet Nâzım Hikmet were destroyed in China's book burning sessions. There is always a problem with a place where people burn books." The anti-intellectual purges targeting bookworms like him further alienated Duran from the Maoist model.

Duran finally parted ways with Turkish Maoists and aligned with Turkey's New Left movement and became Istanbul correspondent for the French-language daily Libération.

Nowadays, Duran notes, China wields soft power in Turkey through different means.

LEFT: Supporters of China's Muslim Uighur minority hold placards as they gather on Beyazid Square in Istanbul in 2020

prosecution of Uighurs," said Çağaptay, adding that Chinese media "has a long way to go before we can say what they do is journalism".

Another irony Duran points out is the case of former English Premier League footballer Mesut Özil.

The Arsenal star published a poem denouncing the treatment of Uighurs in China in December 2019, scolding Muslim countries for their silence about Xinjiang. This earned the ire of China's Central Television which removed the Arsenal-Manchester City match from its schedules. Özil later left Arsenal and signed for Turkey's Fenerbahçe soccer team.

"He opposed the Uighurs' treatment for it insulted his political views," said Duran. "But his stance complicated Özil's ties to Arsenal. Strangely, now that Özil is playing in Turkey, he may not be able to voice the same criticisms."

State and businesses may remain silent, but Turkey's social media is awash with posts depicting the ordeals of Uighurs. "The government is relying on the assumption that it can control the narrative domestically and that this story won't be written because they can tell people in the major media outlets to simply not cover the plight of the Uighurs," Çağaptay said.

But he added that this tactic might not work for much longer.

"The government may control information in conventional media, but they can't control the flow of unconventional media," he said.

The distinction between state and the ruling party, he noted, is vanishing in Turkey. But, despite its democratic flaws, Turkey has not yet morphed into a People's Republic. ⊗

Kaya Genç is contributing editor (Turkey) for Index. He is based in Istanbul

50(01):51/53|DOI:10.1177/03064220211012302

Its Confucius Institute has operated in Istanbul since 2008, conducting Chinese language classes at Boğaziçi and Okan universities. The state-run Xinhua news agency covers Beijing's Turkish investments in areas such as nuclear energy, high-speed rail projects and thermic plants.

China also operates a radio station, CRI Turk, which is mostly staffed by young journalists on short contracts. There is also a Turkish-subtitled Chinese channel, CTV, available on satellite.

In the aftermath of Erdoğan's crackdown on the media, so many Turkish journalists have lost their jobs that foreign outlets such as these can offer a sliver of hope for reporters.

But the Committee to Protect Journalists' latest reports – which show that the only country that jails more journalists than Turkey is China – somewhat dampen such hopes.

"The government turns a blind eye to Chinese-run media in Turkey for the same reason it turns a blind eye to Chinese

 Turkey is trying to appease Beijing in order to continue securing loans from China for its major construction projects

FREE FANG BIN

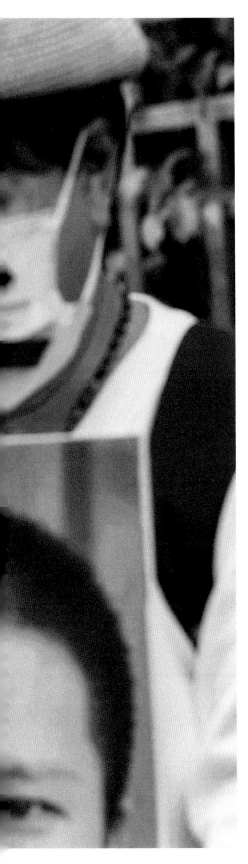

ESSAY

The Human Face and the Boot

Celebrated author **MA JIAN** reflects on the terrible legacy of the Chinese Communist Party in its centenary year

SOMETIMES, FROM THE most trivial event or seemingly insignificant interaction, you can gauge the health of a society and decide: "This is a place I'd like to live, a place conducive to happiness."

A few years ago, while in Taiwan for a literary festival, I went to a night market to look for *tangyuan* – the sticky rice dumplings that are traditionally eaten on the final day of Chinese New Year. As their name is a homophone for the word "union"', Chinese families eat them on this day to ensure that during the coming year they will remain united. As I'd recently been cast into exile from mainland China, I thought the dumplings could assuage my longing for home.

After a long search, I found a small dumpling stall and asked the elderly owner if she had any. She told me she'd sold out, but that if I bought a bag of frozen ones from the supermarket across the road she would boil them up for me on her stove. I did as she suggested and she served them to me in a big bowl, handed me a spoon and invited me to sit at one of her rickety tables. She fervently refused my offer of payment. As I sat there savouring the hot, translucent dumplings stuffed with sweet black sesame paste, I felt closer to home than I had done in years.

It was not the dumplings themselves or the memories they evoked that made me feel close to home. It was the simple

act of kindness from this old woman who didn't know me. Her kindness struck me as peculiarly Chinese. It was imbued with what we call *renqing*: a sentiment, a human feeling that inspires one person to perform a favour for another simply because they can, with no thought of recompense.

Traditional Chinese society was glued together by such sentiments. Their roots lie in Confucian values of benevolence, righteousness and propriety. At the heart of them all is the idea that to lead a good life you must treat others with compassion, that each human being has

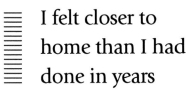

I felt closer to home than I had done in years

the potential to be good and is worthy of dignity and respect. Almost 500 years before the birth of Christ, Confucius devised his own Golden Rule: "When you leave your front gate, treat each stranger as though receiving an honoured guest … Do not do to others what you do not wish for yourself."

But in China, these ancient values have been bludgeoned by 70 years of Chinese Communist Party rule. Since the days of Mao, the CCP has clung to power through violence, propaganda and lies, viewing its subjects as senseless cogs that it can blind with promises of a →

LEFT: A protester demonstrates in support of citizen journalist Fang Bin who posted videos about the coronavirus situation in Wuhan in 2020

→ future Utopia while confining them to a present hell. How easy it is for humans to be stripped of reason by a tyrant's deceit and malice. At 13, having survived the Great Famine caused by Mao's reckless Great Leap Forward campaign, when my siblings and I had had to eat toothpaste and tree bark to stave off starvation, I nevertheless longed to join Mao's party. When he launched his Great Proletarian Cultural Revolution, I was incensed that the class background of my grandfather, who had perished in a Communist jail, disqualified me from joining Mao's Red Guards. The deepest hope of my generation was that after purging China of bourgeois elements, we could travel to Britain and the USA to liberate their populations from the yoke of capitalist oppression and welcome them into the CCP's revolutionary fold.

Slowly, as I witnessed horrific scenes of mob violence, I began to see this march to Utopia for what it was: a dehumanising nightmare that divided people into class categories, pitting one against the other in constant struggle, "rightist" against "leftist", neighbour against neighbour. Time-honoured values of family loyalty and respect for elders were shattered as sons were encouraged to betray their fathers and daughters their mothers. No thought other than Mao Zedong Thought was allowed. Anyone who, however inadvertently, strayed from party orthodoxy was branded a class enemy and destroyed.

At least 45 million people are estimated to have died in Mao's Great Famine. Millions more were killed or persecuted in his Cultural Revolution. Mao's ideas and values caused catastrophic suffering and death, and corroded the hearts of the nation.

In the 40 years since Mao's death, the Chinese have been forbidden to reflect on their traumatic past or contest any current injustices. Like a cunning and obdurate virus, the CCP has mutated. While other communist regimes around the world have fallen, it lives on, still suppressing free thought, still whitewashing history, but embracing, with increasing vigour, the capitalism Mao strove to eliminate. The party has loosened tethers it itself placed on the economy, and the Chinese have got rich. Although it continues to spout

ABOVE: Chinese refugees queue for food in Hong Kong during the famine caused by the Great Leap Forward campaign, 1962

Marxist-Leninist jargon, its overarching obsession is power, and how to cling on to it. It still views the Chinese people as senseless cogs it can manipulate or flatten as it pleases. It still tells them that the material life is all that matters and that happiness is the China Dream of wealth and national glory conceived by the party's current leader, Xi Jinping. Freedom, democracy, human rights, the desire to become master of one's own fate: all of these are unnecessary, absurd, dangerous, it says. The Chinese people have no need for them!

In George Orwell's Nineteen Eighty-Four, Winston is told that if he wants a picture of the future, he must "imagine a boot stamping on a human face – forever".

This totalitarian nightmare is not some fictional future, though. Published in 1949, the year Mao rose to power, the novel prophetically describes China's fate under CCP rule.

For moments, sometimes for days or weeks during the dark decades of China's recent history, a hand has pushed the boot aside and the human face has looked up. It looked up with hope and joy during the Tiananmen Square protests of 1989, when millions gathered across the nation to call for freedom and democracy. In 2008, it looked up when 303 Chinese dissidents signed Charter 08 that argued for an end to one-party rule and asserted that freedom and human rights are universal values that should be shared by all humankind. In Hong Kong, the human face has looked up defiantly as the territory bravely struggles to retain what few freedoms it has left. And last year, back on the mainland, the face looked up for a few short hours when, after Dr Li Wenliang was reprimanded for raising the alarm about Covid-19 and then died of it, Chinese social media became flooded with the courageous hashtag #IWantFreedomOfSpeech.

Every time citizen journalists like Fang Bin upload independent reports on social media, civil rights activists like Xu Zhiyong call openly for political reform, dissidents like Gao Yu shine a light on the secret workings of the oppressive state, the human face looks up and proclaims: "without freedom of speech we are all enslaved".

But each time, the CCP boot stamps back down again. In 1989, it sent the tanks to Tiananmen Square to crush the unarmed protesters. In 2009, it imprisoned the leading dissident Liu Xiaobo who co-authored Charter 08, banned him from collecting the Nobel Peace Prize he was awarded the following year, and in 2017, humiliated him even in death by stage-managing his funeral, forcing his family to drop his ashes unceremoniously into the sea. Fang Bin has been disappeared, Xu Zhiyong is in prison, Gao Yu and countless other dissidents like Ding Zilin, who courageously persists in dragging the Tiananmen massacre from state-imposed amnesia, are under intense surveillance. In Hong Kong, the party has violated the Sino-British Joint Declaration, beaten protesters and arrested every prominent critic. In Tibet, decades of CCP oppression have driven 156 Tibetans to set fire to themselves in anguish.

"But look how much richer the Chinese have become!" CCP apologists cry out. "Western democracies like the USA and Britain are a sham, corrupt and incompetent – see how they failed to contain the Covid-19 epidemic! Does this not prove the superiority of China's authoritarian regime?"

They ignore that the CCP's obsession with secrecy caused the initial outbreak's catastrophic spread, and that democratic Taiwan far outperformed China, recording only 10 Covid deaths, without the government having to imprison whistleblowers or weld Covid patients into their homes.

It's true that UK prime minister Boris Johnson and US president Donald Trump failed disastrously to contain the virus. (Is it a coincidence that both leaders share Xi's disregard for the truth?)

But Trump could be voted out, Johnson can be vilified in the press, and no one loses their freedom of speech. This

The horror of the current situation in Xinjiang is in a category of its own

is the power of democracy – however embattled it may become, it guarantees, more than any other system yet invented, that every citizen can have their say and that political change is always constitutionally possible.

"The Chinese just aren't suited to democracy, though – it's not in their culture," the apologists retort. But Taiwan destroys this argument – it proves that the Chinese can be both prosperous and free.

"It's different on the mainland," the apologists insist. "Look at the popular support for the party!" But the apologists fail to understand that when people have been governed by lies and fear, their gratitude to their leaders is little different from the affection some hostages develop for their captors.

The truth is, everyone in China is a hostage. Some may be wealthier than others, some more aware than others of the prison bars that surround them, but everyone is spiritually incarcerated by the CCP. They have all been denied the most fundamental human right: the right to form independent thought. Without freedom of thought, one loses respect for oneself and the ability to respect and feel compassion for others. China may be rich, but 70 years of CCP rule has plunged the country into an ever-deepening moral abyss.

It is impossible to make a hierarchy of misery, to judge the death and persecution of one person or of one people as worse than those suffered by others. But the horror of the current situation in Xinjiang seems to be in a category of its own. The images of Uighur convicts, handcuffed and blindfolded, heads shaven and bowed, being herded onto trains; of hastily-erected ➔

ABOVE: Dumplings served at a Tapei market in Taiwan, 2018

→ internment camps with watchtowers, barbed wire fencing and high perimeter walls; of inmates forced to smile and sing to foreign inspection teams, despair welling in their eyes; the accounts of torture, rape, forced sterilisations and indoctrination from the few Uighurs who have managed to escape. These images and accounts recall the worst atrocities of the 20th century. In the name of "anti-terrorism", a people and a culture are being annihilated. Determined to eradicate any perceived threat to its rule,

As I witnessed horrific scenes of mob violence, I began to see this march to Utopia for what it was: a dehumanising nightmare

the CCP is stamping its boot down on an entire ethnic group, aiming to extinguish the Uighurs "root and branch".

When reports first emerged of the Xinjiang camps, I found the images too dreadful to bear. Wanting to convey my grief and solidarity, I sought out a Xinjiang restaurant in London, which has now closed. After I paid for my meal, I asked the owner to join me outside, so that we could speak without being overheard. I asked him about the camps, and whether he still had family in the province. It turned out he was not a Uighur but a Han Chinese who had moved to Xinjiang in the 1990s. "Those Uighurs – they deserve what's happened to them!" he said with a smirk. "Good thing they've been locked up in the camps. My family say the streets are much quieter now."

His words were abhorrent, but he was expressing views many Han Chinese on the mainland share. These Chinese mainlanders are not evil, of course. The corrupted moral view that some of them may have is the tragic product of an evil regime.

On the hundredth anniversary of its founding, the CCP will reassert that 'Without the Communist Party, there is no New China!' Xi wants his model of authoritarian capitalism to be applauded and replicated by the entire world. He wants the UN to move its headquarters to Beijing – the ultimate validation of his ideas and values.

For anyone who cherishes human rights and freedom of speech it is repugnant that, while hundreds of millions of victims of the CCP's man-made disasters lie rotting in their graves, while Chinese dissidents continue to be jailed and disappeared, while Hong Kong turns from a place that once offered refuge to mainland dissidents into a place from which its own citizens flee, while Tibetans continue to set themselves on fire, and while a genocide is taking place right now in Xinjiang – it should be repugnant to everyone that in the face of such unending injustice, some Western commentators could suggest that the CCP is winning the battle of values and ideas in the world.

But more appalling still is that for the sake of some grubby trade deals with China, the political leaders of Western democracies are doing little more than offering asylum to Hong Kong citizens and expressing "concern" at China's human rights abuses. As China's economy grows and CCP values spread across the nation's borders, freedom of speech, liberal values and renqing – that essential human capacity for kindness and compassion – will become increasingly endangered. Unless Western leaders defend, not with gunboats or empty rhetoric but with unwavering commitment, the enlightenment values of liberty, fraternity and reason that should form the foundation of every civilised country, then there will soon be very few places left in the world that are conducive to human happiness. ✸

Ma Jian is an award-winning Chinese writer. His latest novel is China Dream. His work is banned in China. Translated from the Chinese by Flora Drew.

50(01):54/58|DOI:10.1177/03064220211012303

A moral hazard

Chinese influence on university campuses is a troubling challenge to free speech, writes **SALLY GIMSON**

THE VICE-CHANCELLOR OF a top UK university was rung up by the Chinese embassy and told to de-platform a Taiwanese politician who had been invited to speak by a professor. The university had close links with China as well as Chinese students. The vice-chancellor complied with the embassy's request and the politician's invitation was rescinded.

This is a story told to Index by Steve Tsang, professor at the China Institute of the School of Oriental and African Studies in London. It was also part of his evidence to a parliamentary committee in 2019 which looked at Chinese and influence on universities in the UK.

It is hard to verify, and Tsang would not name the university, but Tsang says he has no reason to doubt it happened.

ABOVE: Chinese students oppose a Hong Kong pro-democracy protest on Edinburgh's Princes Street, 2019

Being so entangled with the Chinese Communist Party, says Tsang, means that UK universities are creating a "moral hazard".

There has been growing concern in the UK about the influence of the Chinese Communist party in academia and the money that China brings to UK academic institutions.

UK parliamentarians have warned that universities have become dependent on money from the Chinese government and that not enough is being done to guarantee academic freedom. →

> There are worries about whether Chinese students and others at UK universities are free to discuss or express opinions on subjects sensitive to the CCP

Many Chinese students have come to study in the UK because they want to enjoy academic freedom… When you don't give them a safe environment to do that, you are really taking away their right to learn

→ There are worries about whether Chinese students and others at UK universities are free to discuss or express opinions on subjects sensitive to the CCP, such as the genocide of the Uighur minority, Taiwan, the 1989 Tiananmen Square protests, Hong Kong and Tibet. Those concerns have increased following the introduction of the Chinese National Security Law last year which criminalised protests and opposition to the government, not only in China and Hong Kong but abroad as well.

A paper recently published by Civitas, a think-tank, has accused UK universities of not monitoring their relationships with universities in China, and warned that sensitive UK technology may be finding its way into the hands of the Chinese military through joint research projects and sponsorship tie-ups.

They found for instance that Queen Mary University in London had a large joint research centre with Northwestern Polytechnic University, an institution which says it is "devoted to improving and serving the national defence science and technology industry."

At the same time, it was revealed that an Oxford University college had accepted £700,000 (nearly $1 million) to change the name of its chair of physics, naming it after the Chinese technology giant Tencent, which owns WeChat – the app used by more than one billion people in China and whose users are actively monitored by the state. Tencent had also been giving millions of pounds to Cambridge University to fund research.

But it is not just in the UK where there are worries about CCP influence on academics and the effect that is having on free speech and the free flow of ideas. People in other European countries, particularly on the edge of Europe, have similar concerns. In the Czech Republic, the head of the King Charles University's Centre for Security Policy was sacked after the media revealed he billed the Chinese embassy (as well as the university) to run conferences on China. And in January this year, Hungary – which banned the Central European University from operating in the country – announced that it was opening a campus of the Chinese state-run Fudan University in Budapest.

The UK stands out in Europe for the sheer number of students welcomed from China. There are around 220,000 Chinese students at its universities today, bringing with them $5.5 billion of fees – a good proportion of them, according to China-expert Charles Parton of think tank Rusi, paid for directly by the Chinese state.

The last five years has seen an explosion in the numbers and applications – for 2019-20 they were up by 30%. This is in part because countries such as Australia and the USA have become more hostile to the Chinese government. Student numbers at their universities have dropped as bilateral ties have deteriorated. The Chinese government threatened to boycott Australian universities because of a row over the origins of the coronavirus last year, and in the USA 1,000 Chinese students had their visas revoked because they were deemed a security risk.

But universities in the UK have been actively courting Chinese students, encouraged by the government announcing a "golden age" of relations between the two countries in 2015.

Universities also need the money. Public funding for university teaching has gone down by 79% in real terms since 2010. In Scotland, universities do not

ABOVE: Prince Andrew and President Xi Jinping at the opening of the Confucius Institute at University College London, 2015

even have the fees from home students, but are reliant instead on a grant from the Scottish government which has gone down in real terms.

And this reliance on Chinese student income across the UK has meant there has been little scrutiny about how the CCP might try and control its students. Parton told Index for instance that the Chinese embassy funds the Chinese Scholars and Students Associations in the UK which gives students money for "political purposes", such as demonstrating in the streets in support of the CCP.

Many universities are either turning a blind eye to this, or in the case of Strathclyde University actively encouraging it. Their website declares: "The Strathclyde Chinese Students and Scholars Association (SCSSA) is a ➔

→ very active Chinese Students Society registered both in Strathclyde Student Union and Chinese Embassy in the UK. The association is entirely run by Chinese students and its purpose is to serve every Chinese student and scholar in the University of Strathclyde."

Strathclyde has only 1,000 Chinese students, but Edinburgh University had more than 6,300 students from mainland China registered in 2019-20. They bring with them vast fees which make up more than half the £224 million ($310

million) the university receives from non-EU students.

In November 2019, a student from Chengdu who was protesting in the centre of the city with a sign saying he supported Hong Kong students was photographed at the protest and again while putting his mother on a flight home at Edinburgh airport.

Both photos were circulated on Chinese social media site Weibo under the post: "Brothers from Chengdu, beat him to death."

The Covid-19 pandemic has made the situation for those students arguably more difficult because many have not been able to travel to Edinburgh and are studying remotely in mainland China, via a platform which is run by Chinese company Alibaba and has been bought by the university.

Sarah Liu, who lectures in politics at Edinburgh University, has concerns about the use of a Chinese company to allow students to access course material.

"We know that if we use virtual private networks hosted by Alibaba, data routes back to the Chinese communist regime," she said. "This concern is particularly amplified because of the recently passed National Security Law."

Ivana Karaskova, from Prague, is the director of MapInfluenCE, which looks at Chinese influence in central Europe. She is also a lecturer at King Charles University.

She, like Liu is worried about the freedom of expression enjoyed by her Chinese students. She lectures on China and international relations at the university and is noticing now that there are many more students from the Chinese mainland than there are from Hong Kong and Taiwan.

"When I had students from Hong Kong, I quite often experienced that – during the break – Chinese mainland students asked them to go out from the class and told them they were not supposed to say what they were saying," she said.

As a result, lots of students including from China, did not want to participate in class discussions or write on sensitive topics. This in turn affected their grades. She has now restructured her classes to make sure her students send essays to her privately.

She says Czech academia is largely unaware of what is happening and that, although she has tried to raise awareness, there is no concerted action to deal with it.

While Chinese students, and students from neighbouring countries, are a concern for lecturers, one of the other big worries for China-watchers such as Parton is that academics censor

Western campuses rethink their ties

BENJAMIN LYNCH looks at Confucius Institutes around the world, and how Europe, Australia and the USA are reassessing their relationships with them

There are more than 500 Confucius Institutes currently operating at schools and universities around the world.

China claims that the programme exists as a "bridge reinforcing friendship" by offering Chinese language and teaching programmes to students in colleges and universities. Its critics believe it exists as a propaganda tool that reinforces the message of Beijing at the heart of foreign universities.

The institutes offer free teaching to students about China and the Chinese language and are controlled and funded by the Chinese Communist Party. Recently, in response to criticism, they have been run through the Chinese International Education Foundation, an NGO set up to operate all the institutes, in an attempt to avoid the appearance of direct control.

The UK currently has 29 Confucius Institutes, one of the highest number in the world

Professor Salvatore Babones, an expert on China who teaches sociology at The University of Sydney in Australia, wrote in the US journal, Foreign Policy last year: "Confucius Institutes are not so much designed to indoctrinate the students who take their courses as to influence the administrators of the universities that host them. Rising totalitarianism in China has turned the tables on Western universities: instead of spearheading the liberalisation of China, they are uncomfortably vulnerable to

Chinese pressure in the opposite direction."

In recent years, a number of countries have taken steps to try to reduce this influence.

Sweden has closed all its Confucius Institutes amid growing concern about human rights abuses in China and the jailing of Gui Minhai, the Swedish bookseller and poet from Hong Kong.

German universities are also reassessing their relationships with the institutes. Heinrich Heine University Düsseldorf closed its Confucius Institute in 2016 and the University of Bonn and Hamburg University are looking at the situation.

In the USA, the 2019 National Defence Authorisation Act decreed that educational institutions wishing to secure funding for Chinese language programmes as part of their curriculum must not have Confucius Institutes, or must be able to show that Confucius staff members do not have roles as part of federal government-funded Chinese language courses.

More than 70 of the Confucius Institutes in the USA have closed since the act was brought in. Although about 50 still exist, more are scheduled to close.

Australia, too, has sought to limit the reach of China in educational circles. The Foreign Relations Bill passed in December 2020 allows the federal government to veto any agreement made between Australian universities and foreign countries.

themselves because they are worried that if they criticise the government – or even discuss topics which the CCP finds difficult – they will not be able to continue to study the country.

It has been difficult until recently to get concrete examples of the kind of intimidation that academics might experience But in March 2021 the Chinese government imposed sanctions on nine individuals in the UK prohibiting them or their families from going to China. Most were parliamentarians, but one was an academic, reader in Chinese Studies at Newcastle University, Joanne Smith Finley. She along with the others was accused of what the Chinese foreign ministry called "maliciously spreading lies and information" about Xinjiang.

Smith Finley said: "It seems I am to be sanctioned by the PRC [People's Republic of China] government for speaking the truth about the Uighur tragedy in Xinjiang, and for having a conscience. Well so be it. I have no regrets for speaking out and I will not be silenced."

Newcastle University backed her saying: "Academic freedom underpins every area of research at Newcastle University and is essential to the principles of UK higher education. Dr Jo Smith Finley has been a leading voice in this important area of research on the Uighurs and we fully support her in this work."

But not being able to travel to China will make it difficult for Smith Finlay to continue her research.

These threats are compounded by what some who have spoken to Index see as a deep culture of censorship within the Chinese studies sector itself. If people are too critical of the CCP, they are blamed for being anti-Chinese and have very little support from their peers even when they are intimidated, for instance by being followed or having fake emails sent out in their name.

When it comes to science, technology, engineering and mathematical subjects, Parton is even more scathing about UK universities. He says the country is "hiring out its brains to a system that

is intent on producing a very horrific surveillance and repressive internal system and is using much of the research for military improvement".

He highlights Huawei, which has commissioned research from UK universities on "gait technology" – an alternative to facial recognition – allowing people to be recognised from the way they walk.

Many universities in the UK also have tie-ups with Chinese universities, some of which develop highly secretive military technology, and a some even have campuses in China including Nottingham, Birmingham, Edinburgh and Leeds.

Karaskova is also very aware of the attempts to influence academic discourse and, in turn, to influence the elites of European countries to support China and its aims.

It was at her university in Prague that Milos Balaban a professor was sacked for taking money from the Chinese embassy. But what Karaskova found much more problematic was that Balaban "selected students who they thought were promising and recommended them to the Chinese embassy in Prague and the Chinese embassy invited them to China on the Bridge for the Future Programme, which is specifically aimed at central European youth".

Parton argues there should be a rigorous requirement for universities and their staff to reveal all payments and benefits – from direct payments to flights, accommodation and expenses. "This is what MPs or those who work in parliament and government have to do in order to ensure that they are working in the public interest and not for outside interests," he said. "Similarly, it would help ensure that academics are seen to be upholding academic freedom, and also not helping to boost the capabilities of potentially hostile military or repressive forces."

He added that the UK government was working on codes of conduct for universities and tightening up which

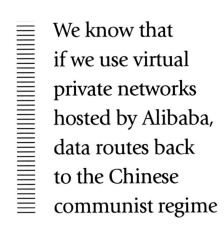

We know that if we use virtual private networks hosted by Alibaba, data routes back to the Chinese communist regime

subjects could be researched jointly with the Chinese.

And Universities UK which oversees universities in the UK told Index: "National security is of the utmost importance to UK universities and every UK university has mechanisms in place to handle risks associated with international research collaborations, in line with government guidance and the values of the UK higher education sector."

Liu believes universities need to concentrate a lot more on the rights to academic freedom of Chinese students themselves.

"Universities shouldn't treat students as a homogenous group as if they all agree or want to comply with CCP censorship," she said.

"That's what a lot of universities do now. They say 'OK, the CCP doesn't allow VPNs, let's find a quick solution' – an easy fix for them. But universities need to remember that many Chinese students have come to study in the UK because they want to enjoy academic freedom. They want to participate, perhaps, in discussions of topics on which they are not allowed to back in communist China. When you don't give them a safe environment to do that, you are really taking away their right to learn." ⊗

Sally Gimson is a UK-based freelance journalist and associate editor at Index

50(01):59/63|DOI:10.1177/03064220211012304

The director's cuts

Sudden changes to the TV schedules at Hong Kong's public broadcaster have caused concerns throughout the industry. **CHRIS YEUNG** reports

RADIO TELEVISION HONG Kong, a public broadcaster, has been in turmoil since a middle-ranking civil servant was given the task of turning the station into a government propaganda machine.

As soon as Patrick Li Pak-chuen took up the post of director of broadcasting at RTHK in early March, he singled out at least three public affairs programmes he needed to review before broadcast. (On the same day, the head of its public affairs programmes and a senior producer resigned, without giving reasons.)

Li's order soon proved to be not just a formality. On 11 March, he made a last-minute decision to drop an episode of the weekly LegCo Review, which would have featured a panel discussion about Beijing's plans for a drastic overhaul of the city's election system. The programme's staff were not given an explanation. They were ordered not to talk about the cancellation to journalists, and warned that doing so might contravene an official secrets law.

The cancellation of the episode came just days after Li dropped an episode

The weakening of the legislature, the judiciary and civil society as a whole has added to the jitters of journalists over media freedom

of Hong Kong Stories, which featured a local writer talking about the ocean and whales. Media reports said the interviewee expressed her sentiments about the 2019 anti-government protests. Again, Li did not explain why the episode was put on hold indefinitely. Production of the remaining episodes has been halted and RTHK staff fear the whole series will be scrapped.

The last-minute cancellation of episodes is anything but usual, deepening the air of anxiety, fear and anger prevalent at the station about the intensified political pressure from the government to interfere with its programmes.

Brutal as Li's cancellation of episodes was, it did not come as a surprise in itself. If there was a surprise, it was the swiftness of Li – a bureaucrat with no journalistic experience – to censor the content of RTHK programmes as soon as he took office.

Li's act of censorship came amidst an orchestrated campaign mounted by China's official media and the local pro-Beijing forces against RTHK. They have lambasted the station for biting the hand that fed it. More importantly, they have accused it of siding with the protesters during the mass demonstrations in 2019 and taking a hostile stance towards the mainland authorities.

The smearing of, and the attack on, RTHK is not an isolated incident. It is part of the intensified campaign spearheaded by Beijing's supporters to try to rein in independent media. By doing so, they are hoping to weaken the power of the media in exercising checks and balances on the power of the authorities.

Superficially, top government officials have given assurances of their commitment to upholding press freedom.

But they have not been shy of venting about their dismay and dissatisfaction about the media.

Late last year, Hong Kong chief executive Carrie Lam said social media had an enduring impact in promoting harmful thoughts among students as she expressed concern that more than 3,000

FROM TOP: Next Media Group founder Jimmy Lai on his way to trial in January 2021; Patrick Li Pak-chuen meets Gladys Chiu Sin-yan, Chairwoman of RTHK Programme Staff Union, March 2021

of them had been arrested since protests broke out in June 2019.

In early February, Lam vowed to bring in new laws to combat doxxing, hate speech and fake news, which she said had proliferated amid the coronavirus pandemic and the social unrest of 2019.

Details of the new legislative initiatives are still unclear at the time of writing. But journalists fear that they are part of the government's game plan to regulate the media by both legislative and administrative means in different names.

Human rights activists and journalists fear that legislative curbs on hate speech and fake news run the risk of being "weaponised" against free speech and a free press. These concerns may not be exaggerated given the prevalence of media-bashing and the erosion of the system of checks and balances.

The fact that the Legislative Council has become increasingly dominated by one camp – the pro-establishment faction, with the Democrats being further side-lined – sparks worries about the representativeness of the whole body. The new legislature will become more "co-operative", rubber-stamping government bills even though some of them may infringe basic civic rights and freedoms.

An independent judiciary is one of the cornerstones of people's rights in Hong Kong. Media freedom is an integral part of the city's freedoms. But political pressure on courts to "co-ordinate" with the executive is mounting.

Under the national security law, the independence of the judiciary is subject to more restrictions. Some judges have come under attack for their rulings, described as being "lenient" over cases related to the 2019 protests. The strength and authority of the judiciary is facing a severe challenge.

The weakening of the legislature, the judiciary and civil society as a whole has added to the jitters of journalists over media freedom that were already prevalent in the wake of the implementation of the national security law last year.

They increasingly feel the intimidating impact of the law since it took effect. The arrest of Next Media Group founder

> It is part of the intensified campaign spearheaded by Beijing's supporters to try to rein in independent media

Jimmy Lai, who is facing a list of charges including subversion, and the raid at its headquarters last year do not augur well for Next or the media in general.

Journalists are getting more sensitive about what they publish – particularly when it comes to video footage that could be considered as subversive. They include the theme slogan of the 2019 mass protest, "Liberate Hong Kong, revolution of the times". Foreign media outlets with offices in Hong Kong are assessing the risks of being based in the city. At least one, The New York Times, has moved some of its operations to Seoul. Other international media outlets are considering similar moves.

Once a vibrant sector in the freewheeling city, a suffocating air of unease and anxiety has engulfed the media in Hong Kong. Journalists, in particular those at RTHK, are facing growing pressure from their management. Self-censorship is getting more serious.

Most journalists remain passionate about journalism. There is no sign of a mass exodus from the industry. But there is also no sign of the end to the darkness which has enveloped the media scene. ⊗

Chris Yeung is a veteran journalist who covers politics in Hong Kong

50(01):64/65|DOI:10.1177/03064220211012305

Beijing buys Africa's silence

China has a hold over Africa, which governments are finding hard to resist, says **ISSA SIKITI DA SILVA**

PICTURED: Entrance to the Congo Dongfang Mining Kasulo mine. Cobalt mined here goes to China for making electronic devices

LEFT: May, 2019. The China Communications Co. project headquarters in Maai Mahiu, Kenya

THE CHINESE-CONGOLESE FRATERNITY hospital stands proud and intimidating in the impoverished township of N'djili, on the outskirts of Kinshasa, capital of the Democratic Republic of Congo.

Opened in September 2007, it is a symbol of the 60 years of co-operation between the Chinese Communist Party and the war-torn Central African nation.

Although the CCP began flirting with the DRC in the 1960s, the relations between the two parties reached a climax in 2007 – during the 18 years President Joseph Kabila's ruled the country with an iron fist – when China signed a controversial resources-for-infrastructure deal, worth \$9 billion.

The deal was vilified at the time by the West, the International Monetary Fund and some NGOs. Chinese companies were to carry carry out infrastructure work: 3,500km of roads, thousands of kilometres of railways, 31 hospitals and 145 health centres.

In exchange, according to Global Business Reports, China would receive 10 million tonnes of copper and 600,000 tonnes of cobalt at an estimated value of \$50 billion over 25 years.

China desperately needs to keep the flame of its affair with the DRC burning because of its myriad natural resources, which include an estimated \$24 billion-worth of minerals and 135 million hectares of rainforest.

Human rights and environmental NGO Global Witness lamented in a 2011 report – China and Congo: Friends in Need – that very little information was publicly available about fundamental financial aspects of the deal.

Local journalists and civil society who scrambled to dig for information about how the Congolese people would benefit met stiff resistance from the authorities, as China's untouchable status in Africa meant nobody was allowed to criticise its omnipresence in Africa. The deal itself was not living up to expectations on the Congolese side with delays and unexpected costs.

"There was, and there is still, very little information about this deal," said Roger, a journalist working for a private media company owned by an ally of the former regime and who did not want to be identified.

"I tried hard to convince my editor at the time to let me do some digging about the deal in order to thoroughly inform the Congolese people how the deal would benefit the whole country. But he categorically refused, citing instructions from the top."

Gideon Chitanga, Africa analyst at the Centre for Study of Democracy at the University of Johannesburg, told Index that China was exporting its culture of authoritarian domestic politics and the muzzling of the press and fundamental freedoms.

"This is done through muting criticism of its deals, [putting a] debt burden on African countries which have no capacity to pay back, and spreading its own media, CGTN, as the major media in Africa," he said.

He added that its media approach was aligned with that of government propaganda from state media in African countries, which did not allow negative coverage of Chinese business deals.

This, he said, entrenched its influence in Africa.

In 2020, a report published by Freedom House – Beijing's Global Megaphone – found a global rise in propaganda, censorship and control of content-delivery systems by the CCP, whose media influence is expanding worldwide.

"Over the past decade, Chinese Communist Party leaders have overseen a dramatic expansion in the regime's ability

In Africa, China is a no-go area when it comes to independent reporting – nobody is supposed to cross that line

to shape media content and narratives about China around the world, affecting every region and multiple languages," according to the report.

"This trend has accelerated since 2017 with the emergence of new and more brazen tactics by Chinese diplomats, state-owned news outlets and CCP proxies."

The report's author, senior research analyst Sarah Cook, said: "Beijing's media influence not only distorts the information environment in the affected settings, it also undermines international norms and fundamental features of democratic governance, including transparency, the rule of law and fair competition."

Propaganda plays a central political role for the CCP, former US national security adviser Robert O'Brien said last year at the White House.

"Over the past decade, the CCP has invested billions of dollars into overseas propaganda operations to great effect and has moved to eliminate 'unfriendly' Chinese language media outlets worldwide, and is close to succeeding," he said.

As China continues its propaganda to convince Africa's leaders that it is the new champion of international justice and peace, dictators seem to have heeded its call – rallying behind it and forsaking the West.

Chitanga said that Africa historically viewed Western relations as politically and economically intrusive and China used the rhetoric of international justice to influence and impact democracy. "African countries identify with the Global South, which historically views Western relations as politically and economically intrusive, because of Western conditionality."

China, which uses the rhetoric of international justice in multilateral relations, wields major leverage in the continent to influence and impact democracy.

"It has focused on protecting its interests and maintaining good relations with African countries at the expense of promoting African voices and media freedoms," Chitanga pointed out.

Criticising China openly about how it conducts its business or foreign policy is like committing suicide, and the African leaders know that

However, China's expansionism in Africa – and its increasingly neocolonialist methods – seems to be dividing the continent's political elite, according to one diplomat, who spoke on condition of anonymity.

"There is a lot of discontent going on behind the scenes within the African political elite. Though they won't say it, or admit it in public, behind the scenes, and in some corridors, many are convinced that China is overstepping its role of trading partner," they said.

Talking about Ethiopia he said: "Chinese companies' ill-treatment of African employees and its disregard for international standards, labour practices and environmental rules is irking many politicians. But they are afraid to raise the issue with Chinese officials for fear of losing financial and political support."

In January 2012, a new headquarters for the African Union – funded by China for $200m – was inaugurated in the Ethiopian capital, Addis Ababa. However, French newspaper Le Monde accused China of spying on African leaders by bugging the building.

"The spying allegations were the last throw of the dice in China-Africa relations, although the continent's leaders chose to sweep it under the carpet so as not to infuriate Beijing," the diplomat said.

"Criticising China openly about how it conducts its business or foreign policy is like committing suicide, and the African leaders know that. As long as China does not interfere in their internal politics, African leaders will continue keeping silent."

China, which wields major leverage in the continent to influence and impact democracy, has focused on protecting its

interests and maintaining good relations with African countries at the expense of promoting African voices and media freedoms," Chitanga outlined.

In the DRC, China turned a blind eye as the Congolese national intelligence agency jailed and tortured thousands of critics of the regime to protect Kabila's government from falling apart.

"China does not engage in public criticism or censure of its partners. Secondly, it is not its policy to do that because it always seeks to protect its economic interests," said Chitanga.

Maintaining its cordial relations with the Kabila regime was a priority, given the wealth in the DRC and the growing Chinese influence in its mining sectors, according to Chitanga

As China enters the stage as the new global power, many observers are wondering whether its silence on freedom and democracy will only become worse.

"Much of these ideas are associated with Western liberal democracy, which is opposed to home-grown state centric developmentalism as practised by China, a mix of state driven authoritarian state capitalism which is extremely politically repressive at home," Chitanga said.

"I'm worried about the future of freedom of expression and other fundamental liberties as the China-Africa co-operation continues to rise," said the diplomat, who urged people to continue to denounce China's oppression of critical voices and its plundering of natural resources.⊗

Issa Sikiti da Silva is an award-winning journalist based in West Africa

50(01):66/69|DOI:10.1177/03064220211012306

A new world order

State-run Xinhua News Agency boasts the largest correspondent network in Africa. As Chinese investors buy stakes in media companies and splash out on advertising, pressure on journalists to report positively on China is mounting. NATASHA JOSEPH reports

IT WAS THE sort of email many journalists send in the digital era: a request for a link as soon as his column – which, that week, focused on China's persecution of more than one million Uighur Muslims in the country's Xinjiang province – went live.

The response Azad Essa received was anything but standard.

"A decision has been taken not to publish your column online this week," an online editor at South Africa's Independent News and Media replied, tersely.

Essa told Index: "I replied asking why and I never received a reply. A few hours later, I received an email saying they had decided to cancel the column because of restructuring. I could, however, pitch occasional op-eds in the future."

Essa is a well-respected and seasoned journalist. At this time in 2018, he worked for Al Jazeera English, covering southern and central Africa, and had published two books. At World's End, his column for Independent, started in 2016.

"My brief was to write about neglected issues of an international nature or interest, but with a specific focus on Africa and the Middle East, if possible. But I have other interests and like to draw comparisons and demonstrate how issues and movements are connected, so I often went beyond that basic brief," he said.

"After a while I could guess the kinds of topics editors liked. But it always went online, so I didn't care too much."

Essa, today a senior reporter for Middle East Eye, said it was not the first time the subject of China had been mentioned as a "sticky point".

"I had previously mentioned China [as] a throwaway line in a column about something else, and it was communicated to me immediately through a staff member that China was a no-go."

The reason? Nobody would say, explicitly. But it is worth noting that 20% of Independent's digital division, IOL, is owned by two Chinese state-owned enterprises: China International Television Corporation and the China Africa Development Fund.

Essa told Index: "I did struggle with the knowledge that they apparently wouldn't want articles on China, but it wasn't like I was bursting at the seams to write about China either.

"I didn't feel like I was being censored because I wrote about the topics that interested me… However, I had decided that should an important or neglected issue concerning China arrive, I would have no choice but to pursue it and that I would confront the purported censorship head-on. So, when the Uighur issue came to light, I wrote about it. I wasn't sure what was going to happen. I figured it was a risk, but this is the job."

The job, it turned out, was over.

Essa's column was canned, and various organisations blasted Independent for its stance.

Reporters Without Borders' East Asia Office director Cédric Alviani said at the time: "This example reflects Beijing's growing influence outside its borders as it seeks to impose a new world media order, by which journalistic ethics and citizens' rights to information would be excluded."

Three years on, its influence has grown in leaps and bounds – and, experts warn, China's enormous investments in African media spaces are bad news for free speech.

ABOVE: South African journalist Azad Essa

Data collated by the China Africa Research Initiative at the Johns Hopkins School of Advanced International Studies in Washington DC shows that China's investment in African countries soared from $75 million in 2003 to $2.7 billion in 2019. In 2014 it overtook the USA in terms of foreign direct investment, becoming the biggest global investor on the continent.

With investment comes influence, and in a virtual panel discussion hosted by the Mercator Institute for China Studies at the end of January 2021, Kenyan journalist Joseph Odindo offered a first-hand account of China's media muscle.

He pointed out that China's state-run Xinhua News Agency boasts the largest correspondent network in Africa. It also offers free content to local news outlets.

Odindo suggested that Kenya had presented itself as a "launching pad" for China's broader African media ambitions. In 2006, Xinhua transferred its regional office from Paris to Kenya's capital, Nairobi.

Odindo told the panel that Xinhua's then-head developed a "very close" relationship with journalists and important media stakeholders in Kenya and "pushed very aggressively for the use of Xinhua content".

This thinking has been echoed by African and Chinese politicians alike. At the 2017 China-Africa Media Forum in Johannesburg, a senior journalist at Zimbabwe's Herald, Tendai Manzvanzvike, was reported by Xinhua as saying that Sino-African co-operation was "necessary to break the Western media monopoly which is meant to suit a particular agenda", adding that co-operation brought opportunities.

Media bosses and Independent's executive chairman Iqbal Survé – an outspoken supporter of China's policies – speak glowingly in public about China. But how do ordinary African journalists experience the Sino-African relationship?

George Ogola is reader in journalism at the University of Central Lancashire in the UK. He has previously worked as a journalist at the Standard in Nairobi and much of his research centres on African journalism. He told Index that journalists he had spoken to perceive China's influence as one of several pressures they face in their daily work.

"Many African newsrooms are particularly financially exposed to economic downturns and the rapid technological changes now increasingly shaping the media landscape," he said.

"China has taken advantage of this vulnerability and uses a number of covert measures to assert its influence.

High advertising spending in a number of African countries is often conditional upon positive coverage of the many projects and businesses China is involved in. Most state media also routinely defer their editorial independence in so far as the coverage of China is concerned.

And it's not just individual journalists

The Chinese are certainly exercising a very harsh type of censorship where they just erase or deny certain things are taking place

who are expected to toe the line.

"Many African newsrooms are aware that Chinese ads, or their largesse – often in the form of training of local journalists or donation of broadcast equipment – is fundamentally conditional on the positive coverage of Chinese projects and investments," Ogola said.

"In Kenya, for example, China withdrew advertising from the Standard newspaper following a critical report of the Chinese-funded Standard Gauge Railway project."

Since his column was pulled, Essa said he had heard stories from other African journalists of "a Chinese style of censorship – rugged and raw and obvious".

Essa argues that in criticising the Chinese, there is an element of double-standards, and that the white Western viewpoint on international affairs which is also promoted in newspapers owned by IOL, can be just as effective at silencing African voices and viewpoints as overt Chinese censorship.

He cites stories reprinted from the British press which are "often a racist, Islamophobic, even xenophobic view of the world on issues and stories that concern the continent like the war on terror or the so-called migrant crisis."

"My point is that censorship is taking place on multiple levels," says Essa. "The Chinese are certainly exercising a very harsh type of censorship where they just erase or deny certain things are taking place, but the alternative often encompasses whitewashing issues under the veneer of liberalism. So, people feel they are free to write what they want – but they aren't really." ✖

Natasha Joseph is a freelance editor and writer based in Cape Town, South Africa. She owns her own company, NCJ Editing

50(01):70/71|DOI:10.1177/03064220211012307

ABOVE: Xinhua News Agency Headquarters in Beijing

A most unlikely ally

STEFANO POZZEBON reports on how the coronavirus pandemic has made Paraguay wonder about dropping its longstanding allegiance to Taiwan in favour of China

N THE CENTRE of Asunción, Paraguay's tropical capital which is roughly the antipodes of Taiwan, a huge avenue cuts through the squared colonial road pattern from east to west.

It's named after Chiang Kai-shek, the Chinese political leader who fled to Formosa at the end of the Chinese civil conflict and founded Taiwan.

The four-lane avenue symbolises, more than any international treaty or trade

agreement, Paraguay's bizarre and long-cemented relationship with Taiwan.

Across the world, only 15 countries still recognise Taiwan as the legitimate Republic of China, and consequently do not have diplomatic relations with Beijing.

Paraguay is the largest of them: friendship ties between the two countries stretch back to the Cold War, when both Paraguay and Taiwan were ruled by fiercely right-wing dictators and most

Latin American nations were not on speaking terms with communist China.

Since those days, China has abruptly entered the world stage, is now the second biggest economy in the world, and for South America in particular, the region's most important economic partner.

Paraguay's ties with Taiwan stand as a remnant of the past, but every year that goes by casts new doubts over the future of this relationship. Last year, at

LEFT: Paraguayan school children wave the Taiwanese flag during a visit from President Tsai Ing-wen

ventilators from China to Argentina, and argued that Paraguay would obtain similar equipment if it switched recognition. The motion was rejected by 25 votes to 16.

Paraguay's oddity as the only nation partnering Taiwan in a region closely tied to China speaks volumes, both inside and outside the country.

The pro-China lobby in Asunción is a variegated front of conflicting interests. It spans cattle ranchers who argue for access to the Chinese market for their products to left-wing politicians who wish Paraguay to be more independent from the USA, and human rights defenders who seem less concerned by the Chinese Communist Party's record of abuse than by Paraguay's internal issues.

One of the most vocal supporters of switching recognition in Beijing's favour last year was Óscar Ayala Amarilla, who serves as director of Paraguay's Human Rights Co-ordinator Group (Codehupy).

Ayala Amarilla told Index the priority last year was to find as much medical equipment as possible in the quickest possible time to protect patients in Paraguay, even though it would have meant recognising an authoritarian regime.

Moreover, not engaging with Beijing because of human rights would be pointless, he said. "I think history has shown that breaking relationships with a country because it violates human rights does not necessarily help with the situation. Just look at Cuba. Every Latin American country except for Mexico decided to quit relationships with Cuba, and 60 years later Cuba is still there and has the same human rights."

Proving just how sensitive the China issue is in Paraguay, Codehupy told Index it did not have an opinion on the question of recognition, and Amaya Amarilla had been speaking in a personal capacity and not representing the organisation he directs.

In 2019, Francisco Urdinez, a professor of international relations at the Pontifical Catholic University of Chile, and his colleague Tom Long calculated the economic cost of Paraguay's relationship with Taiwan. Dubbing it the "Taiwan Cost", they included missed trade opportunities for Paraguayan exports to China and missed investments that Beijing would make in Paraguay if the two countries had a stable relationship.

"It's a question that followed me for months: what is the benefit of sticking with Taiwan?" Urdinez told Index.

Over the past two decades, China has invested billions of dollars in Latin America, from infrastructure loans to building railways and ports, and from seemingly never-ending purchases of soy, minerals and other raw materials to the donation of medical equipment to help cope with the pandemic.

China, which has a huge appetite for copper and beef, is already the leading economic partner of both Chile and Argentina, two countries which share one of the longest land borders in the world but which have little trade with each other. In both countries, the largest exporters are so dependent on Chinese purchases that they have spoken up time and again in support of China in exchange for multimillion-dollar deals that have completely changed Latin America's economies.

Countries linked with Taiwan were excluded from these deals, so Costa Rica, Panama, the Dominican Republic and El Salvador have all switched ➜

the height of the pandemic, a group of lawmakers introduced a motion to the Senate to switch recognition from Taiwan to the People's Republic of China, with the ambition of receiving cheaper and better medical supplies to curb the spread of the coronavirus.

Senators from left-wing parties said switching recognition to Beijing would be pragmatic. Carlos Filizzola, of the Guasú Front, pointed to a donation of

With only a few countries favouring Taiwan, China's goal is finally within reach

China has a huge appetite for copper and beef and is already the leading economic partner of both Chile and Argentina

→ their recognition in the past 15 years as a result of the China's chequebook diplomacy.

While Argentina, Brazil and Venezuela capitalised on the bulk of the investments, Paraguay missed out on it completely: according to Urdinez and Long, Paraguay's Taiwan cost was over 800 million dollars over a 15-year span.

Why does Paraguay stick to its guns over the Taiwan question? Urdinez identifies two reasons.

"This link is almost a familial knot for the hardcore of a handful of the most powerful families of Asunción," he said. "There are ties – symbolic, familial, historical ties – [that are] really strong with Taiwan." When Paraguay's

president Mario Abdo Benitez recently visited Taiwan, he was greeted with pictures showing his father as a member of an official delegation visiting the island four decades earlier.

Secondly, according to Urdinez, there's a more pragmatic reason behind the relationship. "It is very important to be the most important ally Taiwan has," he said. The relationship grants a prominent status to Paraguay, which it can leverage with other partners in the Latin America.

Some of the senators who voted for sticking with Taiwan argued that Paraguay would be lost in the larger mix of Beijing's partners, and that being the biggest fish in a smaller pond was more advantageous to their nation even if at a cost.

Taiwan has shown it cares very much about Paraguay's recognition. In recent years, it has financed a binational

university, built a new parliament building for Paraguay's lawmakers and, in 2020, donated more than one million facemasks as an alternative to Beijing's offers of help in combating Covid-19. But how long Paraguay will be able to withstand China's pressure is anyone's guess.

From Latin America, China wants three things, believes Parsifal D'Sola Alvarado, founder of the Andrés Bello Foundation, a Bogota-based think-tank that specialises in the China-Latin America relationship: raw material exports to feed China's economy, access to the region's markets for Chinese products, and political prestige.

"Winning votes in international forums or multilateral institutions is something China is actively looking for," D'Sola told Index. "The fewer countries criticising China over issues such as Taiwan, Hong Kong or the Uighurs the better, because China really cares about its international image, especially among developing countries."

Among these issues, D'Sola and Urdinez agree that the most important to Beijing is the One China policy, under which Taiwan and mainland China are inalienable parts of a whole, and which envisions a future with Taiwan "reincorporated" into China.

Each country that switches recognition from Taiwan to Beijing is one more step towards achieving that goal. With only a few countries favouring Taiwan, China's goal is finally within reach.

Urdinez believes that Chinese influence in Latin America can expand only in tandem with its economic dominance, and as the number of pro-Taiwan countries dwindles. It means that within Paraguay the same discussion that was had last year will probably be revived sooner or later. Next time, the result might be different. ⊗

Stefano Pozzebon is a regular contributor to Index, covering Latin America. He is based in Bogotà, Colombia

BELOW: Paraguay's President Mario Abdo Benitez and Taiwan's Foreign Minister Joseph Wu with Taiwanese business leaders in October 2019

50(01):72/74|DOI:10.1177/03064220211012308

China's artful dissident

MARK FRARY profiles Badiucao, the artist whose work appears on the cover of this issue of Index

BADIUCAO CALLS HIMSELF a "Chinese-Aussie artist hunted by the Chinese government".

It is easy to see why.

Born in Shanghai, Badiucao was training to be a lawyer when he became a convert to activism. He was watching a pirated Taiwanese film with friends and, unbeknown to them, the film had the documentary about the 1989 Tiananmen massacre, The Gate of Heavenly Peace, spliced into it. The die was cast.

Later, recalling the incident to news agency AFP, he said: "It was three hours, everybody just sat there and the room was completely dark. Nobody even got up to turn on a light."

None of them had ever heard of the events in Tiananmen Square and their horrific conclusion because of Chinese censorship.

Badiucao emigrated to Australia in 2009, abandoning his plan to become a lawyer. After his arrival, he worked as a kindergarten teacher while he studied for a master's degree in education. He began using his artistic talent in his spare time and, in 2011, started drawing political cartoons, becoming a nagging thorn in the CCP's side.

Badiucao had no formal art training in China but comes from a long line of

> ## Badiucao's art is typified by the clever reworking of communist propaganda imagery

creatives – his grandfather and great-uncle were filmmakers in China who paid for their work with their lives in the 1950s.

Badiucao's art is typified by the clever reworking of communist propaganda imagery, subverting it to criticise the CCP and using the bold red and yellow of the Chinese flag. His work uses dark humour and clever wordplay to skewer China's leaders.

In 2018, he worked as an assistant to Chinese artist Ai Weiwei in Berlin and, in November that year, was planning the first solo exhibition of his work in Hong Kong. However, his cover was blown and, because of threats to his family in mainland China, he was forced to cancel.

The following year, China's Artful Dissident, a film by Australian director Danny Ben-Moshe, documented the cancellation of the exhibition. At the end of the film, Badiucao revealed his true identity; he did so because it was clear that the Chinese government already knew who he was. Like many dissidents, he was forced to cut off contact with his family in China in order to protect them.

Index held a special invitation-only screening of the documentary at the Tate Exchange in London with Badiucao in October 2019.

He irritated the Chinese government further that year – the 30th anniversary of the Tiananmen massacre – by creating three designs for a hashflag emoji for Twitter to use on its platform. In the end they were not taken up. In his message to Twitter he said: "Twitter plays such an important role in providing Chinese people to have a free-speech sanctuary above China's Great Fire Wall." But Twitter refused to take up his offer of new emojis

He also annoyed the government in 2020 by writing a daily Wuhan diary,

ABOVE: Cartoonist Badiucao

starting in March, about the outbreak of the pandemic.

His recent work includes repurposed images of Tiananmen's Tank Man and Hong Kong's Umbrella Movement, melded with representations of the instantly recognisable spikes of the Covid-19 virus.

President Xi Jinping and Hong Kong chief executive Carrie Lam are frequent targets of his sharpened drawing tools. Winnie the Pooh, banned in China after comparisons were made between Xi and the illustrated bear, is also a frequent subject.

Badiucao's cover illustration for Index is typical of his work – striking and with a strong message to those who gaze upon it, reminding us of the West's complicity in China's rise to power. ✪

Mark Frary is an associate editor at Index

50(01):75/75|DOI:10.1177/03064220211012309

ESSAY

Lies, damned lies and fake news

NICK ANSTEAD, the author of a new book about misinformation suggests some practical solutions

THE IDEA OF "fake news" and a variety of related concepts (including "post-truth", misinformation and "alternative facts") has become central to the discussion of politics in recent years. Concerns about the issue have been raised around the world. Prominent examples include the USA, particularly following Donald Trump's lie-fuelled presidential election victory in November 2016; and the UK, following the vote to leave the EU in June of that year.

These examples are high profile, but in many countries the problem of fake news existed long before 2016. Citizens of Russia, parts of central Europe and the Philippines would recognise lots of the tendencies that we now associate with fake news. Post-2016, we have seen similar patterns in other countries, including in large democracies such as Brazil and India.

When we consider fake news, the first question that needs to be asked is deceptively complex: what exactly do we mean by the term? In an article published in Nature in 2018, a group of prominent social scientists suggested fake news was

> ## The first question that needs to be asked is deceptively complex: what exactly do we mean by the term?

"fabricated information that mimics news media content in form but not in organisational process or intent".

This definition seems straightforward. However, things become more complicated when we look at other uses of the term. At a press conference during the 2016-17 presidential transition period, Trump responded to a CNN reporter who was questioning him by saying "You're fake news". In 2018, the Trump White House created the Fake News Awards. The top 10 list included organisations such as The New York Times, Time and ABC News and largely consisted of reporting errors that had already been corrected.

Things such as the Fake News Awards have led to considerable pushback against the term. In the UK, a parliamentary committee found that it had "taken on a variety of meanings, including a description of any statement that is not liked or agreed with by the reader", and as a result the term had ceased to be useful.

In reality, it is being used in two distinct ways, which need to be disambiguated. The first definition relates to the spreading of fabricated news-style content. We can think of this as "fake news as misleading content". The second definition relates to when political leaders use it as a rhetorical device to attack those they perceive to be their political opponents, particularly in the media. This is "fake news as populist discourse".

The tension between these two definitions becomes apparent when they generate seemingly contradictory rhetoric. This happens if a populist political leader uses fabricated content to accuse a reputable news organisation of spreading inaccurate information. This occurred, for example, in the aftermath

ABOVE: The Vote Leave campaign bus before the Brexit referendum in May 2016

of Trump's inauguration ceremony, when the size of the crowd attending was disputed. Inaccurate, inflated figures about crowd size were being circulated. As a result, media organisations tried to use reputable methods and sources to provide more accurate figures. They were then promptly accused of lying by the Trump administration.

Can these two seemingly contradictory definitions of fake news be reconciled? If we look at it from a different perspective, these two distinct ideas become part of a single problem. We need to think of fake news as an institutional challenge, created by the declining democratic legitimacy of people who have traditionally been looked at to structure and impose boundaries on political debate: most obviously the newspaper editor and the television journalist.

We should be careful to avoid what is sometimes called "golden ageism". News coverage was not perfect in the past. What is sometimes called the mainstream media has rarely been a paragon of virtue. However, it is also undoubtedly the case that the relative decline of mass media such as newspapers and broadcast television and their replacement with increasingly personalised news content has dramatically changed the way we get information. This is most obviously true of social media, but it is also the case with the growing number of television channels that viewers can choose from.

It is this context which shapes the problem of fake news. The first version of fake news – fake news as misleading content – is powerful because information can circulate more freely and news agendas are more porous. The second form – fake news as populist discourse – is effective precisely because it is often aimed at institutions (such as broadcasters or the traditional media) that are struggling to retain their legitimacy and authority.

Understanding fake news in this way allows us to address another question frequently raised about the problem: haven't politicians always lied? And

if they have, why are we suddenly so concerned about fake news?

Falsehood has long been a part of politics, and we can find examples going as far back as Ancient Greece and Ancient Rome. However, it is the distinctive institutional dimension to fake news that gives it contemporary relevance.

This definition also points towards some possible solutions to the problem, and individuals can certainly do things to protect themselves. Don't share things without reading them first (on social media, you often see only the headline). Think about the provenance of a story. Do you know the news organisation that is posting it? Have you seen the same story on other, reputable news organisations? Do individuals or organisations sharing content have any partisan or ideological biases? These core media literacy skills have never been more vital.

However, these approaches can only

ever offer partial solutions, as they are overly focused on individual news consumers. Instead, we need to be more ambitious and think about how we can reimagine the media and political environment to make it fit for purpose in the 21st century. How do we create environments where people can encounter a diverse range of ideas representing different strands of thinking in society? How can those ideas can be tested through pluralistic debate, and in such a way that debate does not rapidly descend into partisan trench warfare? In short, the only way to fix the challenge of fake news is a renewed political culture. ⊗

Nick Anstead is an associate professor at the Department of Media and Communications at LSE in the UK. What Should We Do About Fake News? is published by Sage

50(01):76/77|DOI:10.1177/03064220211012310

Censorship? Hardly

US publisher **CLIVE PRIDDLE** argues that governments are the real threat to freedom of expression

O N 8 JANUARY 2021, publisher Simon & Schuster decided to cancel the contract of Senator Josh Hawley because two days earlier he had been photographed giving a supportive fist salute to the protesters who were about to invade the US Capitol building in Washington. Was this censorship? Hardly.

I don't know the details of the contract between the publisher and the author, nor have I read the manuscript of the book, so I can't know the grounds for the cancellation. Publishers' contracts often contain "morals clauses" that give them the right to walk away from authors who have done something embarrassing in public. Supporting protesters on the verge of a riot at the

Capitol, however, was not the kind of event those clauses were anticipating.

But Simon & Schuster's decision wasn't censorship for long, if at all. Within a few days Hawley's book had an opportunistic new publisher and will appear in May, after a negligible delay. The public will be able to enjoy his thoughts on tyranny and technology. He will no doubt be present on those parts of the review media that prize his opinions, and it's hard to see how Simon & Schuster's decision has denied the world access to the senator's wisdom.

In fact, it's hard to see how it would be possible to censor any US senator, never mind Josh Hawley in particular. Senators, like many prominent business and public figures, occupy a position

of considerable privilege. The media needs them and offers them pretty much unfettered access. Publishers buy their books less because of what they have to say than because of who the authors are; they are essentially celebrity books.

Readers buy them as an act of tribute. Perhaps the books are read for the power of their ideas, but in a very partisan world many are bought as loyalty totems.

Publishers are optional, anyway. Donald Trump Jnr had a publisher for his book, Triggered, in 2019, but in 2020 he went solo with Liberal Privilege, using Amazon's ebook and audiobook platforms without the involvement of a traditional publisher. That was his choice. We don't know what motivated it, but it clearly wasn't fear of censorship.

Censorship needs to be applied broadly to be worthy of the name. Only a government or state really has the power to ban speech

Publishers might be assumed to be supporters of uninhibited rights to publish. But that is something of an anachronism. The days of liberal-minded people lining up to support the publication of Lady Chatterley's Lover are long gone; you can get 50 shades of sex or gardening on 50 different platforms.

Instead, publishers are having to confront their awkward role as cultural gatekeepers. The gatekeeper idea required a broad cultural consensus – only with that you could plausibly say that people of a certain education and taste might be a useful cultural sieve, one that elevated the best and turned away the rest.

But as our consensus has collapsed – and we are aware that education is a vexed and often inequitable experience, and taste has become a synonym for snobbishness or prejudice or simply one person's egotistical opinion – the possibility that publishers might provide a generally beneficial role as cultural stewards has dissolved. At least in public.

Privately I'm sure many of us still enjoy the fact that we influence what gets published, but we can't kid ourselves. Book publishing used to be expensive, laborious and complicated – beyond the means of most authors. Publishing now can take place without a printed book at all, but even that is much easier to engineer.

The large publishing companies – Penguin Random House, HarperCollins, Macmillan, Simon & Schuster and my employer, Hachette Book Group – have largely abandoned any descriptive claims for what they do beyond offering platitudes about good books.

But good for whom – and how – is left vague. They focus on the number of authors and the range of genres and the prizes won. There's something to distract everyone; no one need linger over the awkward question about what ethos the publisher might have and who might be excluded, deliberately or not, from its lists.

That attitude has, in the last two years, come back to bite publishers because even if they like the moral fogginess, many of their employees do not. Some staff, often the younger ones – but increasingly up the age range as older colleagues are emboldened by the example of their younger peers – are not prepared to work in an ideological void.

They want to associate professionally with writing and writers they support. And they can be very vocal in denouncing those they do not like.

When Woody Allen's memoir was acquired by one of the Hachette Book Group publishers but the impetus to abandon the publication came not from the top but from the collective feeling among many employees, some quite junior, that they did not want to be associated with it. And that view prevailed. Allen had allegations of sexual abuse made against him by his daughter Dylan Farrow in the 1990s. He protested his innocence and went through the US courts who cleared him.

So was that a form of mob censorship? Again, not at all. The book found another publisher instantly – you can buy it right now on Amazon. Foreign language editions are also available so in no way has Allen been censored. He was dropped, but his First Amendment rights to free speech were not offended.

In an age of so many platforms for so many views, the whole idea of First Amendment rights being under threat seems almost quaint. Instead it is the unfettered proliferation of opinions, well-founded or bogus, that is the challenge. And the conversation about censorship has moved away from traditional book publishing and onto social media platforms, where the fake news provocations provide the spark to the tinder.

Disinformation, distortion, distraction and diversion are all having a field day: so much so that we can be fairly sure that censorship is really not in play. At least not in the USA. In China, Russia, Saudi Arabia and among the usual autocratic suspects, it is a different world.

Some of the anger directed towards Allen was because he was an old white man, a category of author that has historically received a generous amount of publishing's time, attention, flattery and money. For many, the indulgence of a tainted author was a step too far when so many deserving writers struggle to get their start.

The statistics here are clear: publishing disproportionately favours white authors over non-white, men over women and, if the data were available, I'm sure they would show that publishing favours the affluent over the poor by the greatest margin of all.

Access to publishing is a problem the industry has only belatedly begun to try to solve. It is complicated. Book publishing is, by definition, a written culture that favours writers of style and control.

Not everyone is equally able, but does that mean that some perspectives and opinions are excluded? Often, yes.

Does it mean educational disadvantage can be excluding? Yes, it does.

Does it mean that some elite writers end up as proxy voices for groups to which they don't belong? Yes, indeed.

Is all this censorship? Not quite.

Oral culture is booming on YouTube and in the blossoming world of podcasts, so the primacy of the written message is certainly being challenged, as it should be. But under-representation in publishing of the non-elite, however you define it, is conspicuous.

If it is to change significantly and lastingly, it will require more than an industry mindset to change. The ➡

→ education system in the UK and US needs to be retooled to serve better the disadvantaged; and the valuation of arts education will have to improve so that as an industry we can pay a viable wage for those dependent on it and without other means of financial support. Steps in that direction have been taken; more will be needed.

In some ways it is surprising that someone like Hawley wants to be published by a company such as Simon & Schuster. There is, of course, the money. He will have received a sizable advance payment for his book, which is a reminder that all large publishers are commercial operations and the need to act effectively as businesses is paramount.

Publishers' preferences are usually driven by what they think they can sell. To pay the salaries and the benefits to their staff they must be profitable. They are entitled to make their own minds up about which books are attractive business propositions.

Hawley's book was deemed a commercial opportunity. Then, it wasn't.

Time will tell which judgment was right.

New York governor Andrew Cuomo received a seven-figure advance from the Crown publishing group at Penguin Random House for his book about leadership during the Covid-19 crisis. It printed a large number of copies – an apparently excessive number because by the time the book appeared, Cuomo's leadership looked less exemplary.

Covid-19 numbers in New York state care homes were much worse than he had suggested, and then a number of women – nine at the time of writing – came forward to accuse the governor of unethical workplace sexual misdemeanours.

Crown declared it would not reprint the book, or issue a paperback edition. We don't know if this was an ethical or a business decision – when Crown made it there was no consumer demand for further printings or editions of the book.

Either way, the decision was certainly not censorship.

Money aside, the value that Simon & Schuster and the other major publishing houses bring to the Hawleys and Cuomos is a vague sense of glory by proximity: it's easy to see how Cuomo would love to be at the same publisher as Barack Obama, or Hawley alongside Ernest Hemingway, but let's be honest – Cuomo is, in writerly terms, no Obama, and while I still haven't read the Hawley book I suspect the Bell does not Toll for him as a literary stylist.

Before it became part of the American canon, For Whom the Bell Tolls *was* banned by the US Post Office, which declared it non-mailable because of its alleged communist sympathies. While it didn't make the book entirely unavailable, it was a ban by a state agency, and that gets to the heart of censorship.

Censorship needs to be applied broadly to be worthy of the name. Only a government or state really has the power to ban speech – although the transnational reach of Facebook and Google and Microsoft gives them very potent powers of influence over online conversation and the exchange of opinion, far greater than should make the rest of us feel comfortable. But reassuringly none of those companies can censor a book entirely, yet.

Hawley protested (on Twitter) when his book was dropped by Simon & Schuster (see below).

His view is high-falutin' horse shit. Orwell wouldn't touch it.

The idea that "only approved speech can be published" is dismissed by evidence to the contrary everywhere. The conservative Fox News presenter Sean Hannity was high in the bestseller lists when Hawley made his remarks – somehow he had escaped the apparent Orwellian cancel culture.

"Culture" is not the state. Public opinion can affect how books are perceived and distributed; it very rarely gets close to banning them, making them genuinely unobtainable or erasing their content.

When Hawley says he intends to fight his non-existent opponent with everything he has, he ironically gets close to revealing a truth. People such as him have a great deal – they have power, access and opportunity, and usually they are well funded.

Hawley likes this fight not because he's taking on a real opponent but because it's a mirage. The state hasn't tried to ban the junior senator for Missouri. Of course it hasn't. L'Etat, c'est lui, after all, and he knows it. ⊗

Clive Priddle is the publisher of PublicAffairs, part of the Hachette Book Group in the US. He was previously publishing director at HarperCollins UK and Fourth Estate

50(01):78/80|DOI:10.1177/03064220211012311

Josh Hawley
@HawleyMO

My statement on the woke mob at @simonschuster

This could not be more Orwellian. Simon & Schuster is canceling my contract because I was representing my constituents, leading a debate on the Senate floor on voter integrity, which they have now decided to redefine as sedition. Let me be clear, this is not just a contract dispute. It's a direct assault on the First Amendment. Only approved speech can now be published. This is the Left looking to cancel everyone they don't approve of. I will fight this cancel culture with everything I have. We'll see you in court.

11:42 PM · Jan 7, 2021

♡ 112K   ○ 282.8K   ↑ Share this Tweet

A voice for the persecuted

On Index's 50th anniversary, chief executive **RUTH SMEETH**, finds it more important than ever to champion free speech and expose censorship all over the world

FIFTY YEARS AGO, on the 25th March 1971, four visionary people came together to sign the founding deeds of the Writers and Scholars International, the original publishing vehicle for the magazine in your hands today. Elizabeth Longford, Peter Calvocoressi, Stuart Hampshire and Stephen Spender. We were blessed with our founders, they were eminent, determined and staunch defenders of the right of free expression around the world. They were also unrelenting in their opposition to totalitarianism wherever it existed. They collectively recognised the threat of authoritarian regimes to our collective repository of knowledge. When great thinkers and artists have no place to make their arguments, to showcase their work, to challenge convention, we all lose.

Their objective therefore was to provide a voice for the persecuted. As Stephen Spender wrote upon our launch in The Times newspaper:

"…if a writer whose works are banned wishes to be published, and if I am in a position to help him to be published, then to refuse to give help is for me to support the censorship. If I complacently accept the idea that freedom is something that happens in some places and is prevented in others, I am implying that freedom is a matter of accident, or privilege, occurring — if I happen to have it — at the place where I live. This attitude to freedom really undermines it, for it is to support the views of those who hold freedom to be a luxury enjoyed by bourgeois individualists."

Over the last half century, we have sought to live up to the vision outlined by our founders. We've featured the

works of inspirational dissident writers from Vaclav Havel to Salman Rushdie and Ma Jian. We've covered every aspect of censorship throughout the world from journalists being assassinated to governments restricting access to the internet. We've run successful campaigns on issues as varied as libel reform in the UK to hate speech. We've exhibited the work of artists and writers from repressive regimes at the Tate Modern and the British Library. We've featured the plays of Tom Stoppard and Samuel Beckett. And we've supported over 80 Freedom of Expression award winners in the last 20 years. I am so proud of what our small team of dedicated journalists, activists and campaigners has achieved, supported by some inspirational trustees and generous financial backers. I wish that on our 50th birthday I was able to announce that we had completed our job and no one was threatened by their government for challenging the status quo or demanding media freedom. Unfortunately, that simply isn't the case.

From Hong Kong to Myanmar, from Belarus to Egypt, from Iran to Kashmir people are being censored. The principles of free expression, the right to protest, the right to freedom of association are being quashed and while the world looks on in horror, there is little action. Index exists to bring hope and to ensure that the targets of censorship have a home for their voice to be heard.

In the coming months as we mark our 50th birthday it is our goal to use our unique platform to ensure people can tell their stories. We have launched in partnership with Times Radio a "Letters from Home" series so that our correspondents can tell their own stories

ABOVE: Clockwise from top left: Poet Stephen Spender, codebreaker and historian Peter Calvocoressi, biographer Elizabeth Longford and philosopher Stuart Hampshire

and to mark our birthday we have rebranded and redesigned the magazine. I hope you like it. We have huge plans for the coming months, from new art projects inspired by our magazine archive to exciting projects on climate change and soft power. We can only do all this work because of your support. Thank you.

Every day we seek to live up to the vision laid out by our founders: to be a voice for the persecuted. ✪

Ruth Smeeth is chief executive of Index on Censorship

50(01):81/81|DOI:10.1177/03064220211012312

"Impassioned,
scholarly and
succinct "

The Times

Free
Speech

And Why It Matters

Andrew
Doyle

CULTURE

What laughter and comedy has always done is to take
power away from people and knock them down to size

SHALOM AUSLANDER ON HIS NEW SHORT STORY ANTI-HA | DON'T JOKE ABOUT JESUS P84

Don't joke about Jesus

SALLY GIMSON talks to American author **SHALOM AUSLANDER** about laughter and the power to subvert

SHALOM AUSLANDER LIKES to shock. His latest novel, Mother for Dinner, is about a family of cannibals. It's funny, outrageous and a bitter critique on US society and identity politics.

The book is a long joke and the plot is based on William Faulkner's As I Lay Dying. Auslander is attracted to the idea of writing the great American novel, but he also feels the idea is too serious.

His previous work was called Hope: A Tragedy, about Anne Frank ageing and geriatric in an attic in New England, writing furiously.

It won the Jewish Quarterly-Wingate Prize in 2013 and was named by The Times in London last year as "possibly the funniest novel of the decade".

Creating humour out of the taboo is Auslander's trademark.

"For me, laughter and comedy were a lifesaver – they are why I am still alive," he told Index. "I'd have offed myself a long time ago if I couldn't laugh."

Auslander was born into an ultra-orthodox Jewish family in Monsey, New York, which he has also written about in his memoir, Foreskin's Lament.

It is this upbringing which has inspired much of his work – the rituals and religion he rebelled against but is still attracted to, and in which he finds comfort.

The original short story he has written for Index, which we publish here, is a ritual joke which Auslander subverts, to challenge our sense of humour and readiness to be offended.

The story ends with the most basic joke of all. Twenty years ago, said Auslander, if he had been called by Index to write a short story he would have thought he should write something "serious and heavy" about voices being shut down.

"And now I find the thing people most aren't allowed to say, the thing people get

most cancelled for, is a joke which I know would be funny if it were fiction, but if it's something you actually have to live in it's much less funny."

Auslander's heroes, apart from Faulkner, are Samuel Beckett and Franz Kafka – "who were funny about the darkest of things" – Flannery O'Connor and Kurt Vonnegut. Stand-up US comedians Bill Hicks and Lenny Bruce are also important to him "and suffered". Hicks's routine was cut from David Letterman's TV show in 1993 because of jokes about anti-abortionists and religion. He died of cancer shortly after.

Auslander is now living in California with his family because, he says, his British wife wanted the good weather. His targets are not just right-wing, populist adherents of former US president Donald Trump but leftists, of whom he was once one but who he now accuses of having lost their sense of humour.

"I grew up left wing and it was always the right wing which were saying 'Don't joke, watch what you say, don't joke about Jesus, don't joke about God and abortion isn't funny', and my heroes – whether they were novelists or comedians or artists – were always on the left, laughing. Now it's like everyone says you are not allowed to laugh about anything." He sees a USA where people are divided because the voice of "the lunatics" is amplified.

"If you listen to the loonies on either

side – which is all the media, including the social media – you believe we all want to hang each other or kill each other. The reality is 99% of us agree with 99% of things. We are not particularly divided about issues. We are just being led around by the lunatics.

"One of the things lunatics hate is laughter: they hate jokes. What laughter and comedy has always [done] is to take power away from people and knock them down to size."

He added that it used to be said that the first things fascists did when they came into power was to kill the wits, the writers and the comedians.

"That was the first thing they did, kill them all, because they knew [the wits, the writers, the comedians] had the power to cut them all down."

Auslander is an evangelist for laughter. He quotes Faulkner again in an introduction to a collection of stories by Sherwood Anderson saying that humour was a critical part of culture and who Americans are.

He says also he read that writers who wrote with a smile eventually get taken seriously. "My hope," he told Index, "is that it's the opposite: that writers who write seriously with their head in their hands eventually get laughed at."

Auslander is a contrarian. He wants the serious to be challenged but he does want to be taken seriously. He reflects ruefully that he would have more awards

> Humour and laughter is saying 'We are not all that great, we are pretty silly', whereas tragedy tries to make us all noble, which we are not

if he moved people to tears. Instead, he finds that he is writing books that are well-received, but sometimes too difficult for popular consumption.

He said he thought Americans found the issues in Mother for Dinner particularly hard to talk about.

He doesn't know which is worse, being insulted for what he writes or that people are unwilling even to talk about his work.

"In some ways that's the more irritating one – to hear back from media of any kind, 'Well, we really liked it, but we can't talk about it'. That just makes me angry because I know these people in three weeks' time are going to be on an interview somewhere, patting themselves on the back for being bastions of free speech."

Auslander says that "after years of therapy" he still wakes up in the morning feeling tragic, but he doesn't want more tragedy in his life.

Laughter, he says, comes from being

> Now I find the thing people most aren't allowed to say, the thing people get most cancelled for, is a joke which I know would be funny if it were fiction, but if it's something you actually have to live in it's much less funny

oppressed, and the funniest people in the USA today are no longer Jews but Latinos and African Americans, "because they are suffering the most".

But most of all, Auslander sees laughter as reflecting the absurdity of the human condition.

"Humour and laughter is saying 'We are not all that great, we are pretty silly', whereas tragedy tries to make us

all noble, which we are not. We are all laughable, and I find great comfort in that. It probably makes for a better future if we understand we are all just a bunch of assholes, and that's funny."

Sally Gimson is a UK-based freelance writer and an associate editor at Index

50(01):84/89|DOI:10.1177/03064220211012313

Anti-Ha

by SHALOM AUSLANDER

A MAN WALKS into a pub and sits down at the bar. At the table nearby sit a rabbi, a priest and a nun with a parrot on her shoulder.

The bartender eyes them.

He doesn't want any trouble.

The man's name is Lipschitz, and he doesn't want any trouble either. It's been a long day, looking for a job, any job, but to no avail. Once upon a time he could earn a hundred dollars a night, at pubs much like this one, delivering his comedy routine to a joyful, appreciative crowd. But that feels like a long time ago. Now he just wants a drink. He would sit somewhere else if he could, well away from the possibility of a joke, but it is Friday night and the pub is full. For a moment

he considers leaving. The bartender comes over.

"What can I get you?" the bartender asks.

Lipschitz glances at the table nearby.

The rabbi sips his scotch. The priest checks his phone. The nun orders a cranberry and soda.

"Just a beer," says Lipschitz.

The parrot says nothing.

Nobody laughs.

Phew.

* * *

A beautiful blonde woman walks into a pub and sits down at the bar.

The woman's name is Laila. She is of Islamic descent on her father's side, and she sits at the bar beside Lipschitz, who is of Jewish descent on his mother' side.

There's nothing funny about that. The Arab-Israeli conflict has led to the loss of countless innocent lives.

➔

The parrot is being judgmental, and is only considering the man's actions from its own privileged heteronormative perspective

→ The bartender comes over.

"What can I get you?" he asks.

Laila orders a martini.

She glances over at the rabbi, the priest and the nun with the parrot on her shoulder. Laila has a devilish glint in her eye, a certain mischievous sparkle that Lipschitz finds both alluring and troublesome.

"Well," she says with a smile, "it's better than a parrot with a nun on its shoulder."

Uh-oh, thinks Lipschitz.

He doesn't want any trouble.

The bartender, a young man with a ponytail and a scruffy goatee, casts a watchful eye over them. He wears a brown T-shirt with the words HUMOR LESS in large white letters across the front. Lipschitz had seen such shirts before – and the hats and the hoodies and the laptop stickers. The first time he saw it was a year ago, at what was to be his very last nightclub performance. He had made a joke about his mother, and a man in the front row, wearing the same shirt, stood up and began to heckle him.

"Boo!" the man shouted. "Mother jokes are weapons of the patriarchy designed to minimise the role of women in the parenting unit!"

Jokes and jest were the latest targets in the global battle against offence, affrontery and injustice. The movement's founders, who proudly called themselves Anti-Ha, opposed humour in all its forms. They did so because they believed, as so many philosophers have, that jokes are based on superiority. Plato wrote that laughter was "malicious", a rejoicing at the misery of others. Aristotle, in his Poetics, held that wit was a form of "insolence". Hobbes decreed that laughter is "nothing else but sudden glory arising from a sudden conception of eminency in ourselves", while Descartes went so far as to say that laughter was a form of "mild hatred".

The heckler stormed out of the club, and half the audience followed him.

"Laughter," read the back of his T-shirt, "Is The Sound of Oppression."

The movement grew rapidly. In New York, you could be fined just for telling a riddle. A woman in Chicago, visiting a friend, stood at the front door and called, "Knock knock!" and wound up spending the night in jail. In Los Angeles, long the vanguard of social progress, a man on Sunset Boulevard was recorded by a concerned passer-by laughing to himself as he walked down the street. The outraged passer-by posted the video online, where it instantly went viral and the man could no longer show his face outside. The subsequent revelation that the man suffered from Tourette's Syndrome, and that his laughter was caused not by derision or superiority but by a defect in the neurotransmitters in his brain, did little to change anyone's mind. No apologies were given nor regrets expressed; in fact, the opposition to humour only increased now that it was scientifically proven that laughter is caused by a brain defect, and "#Science" trended in the Number One spot for over two weeks.

Laila nudges Lipschitz.

"Hey," she whispers. "Wanna hear a joke?"

Lipschitz stiffens.

"It's a good one," she sings.

Lipschitz knows she's trying to tempt him. He knows he should head straight for the door. But it's been a rough day, another rough day, and the booze isn't working anymore, and soon he'll have to go home and tell his mother and sister that he didn't find work – again – and so in his languor and gloom, he looks into Laila's dancing green-flecked eyes and says, with a shrug, "Sure."

Laila leans over, hides her mouth with her hand and whispers the joke in his ear.   →

→ The rabbi and the priest discuss God.

The nun feeds her parrot some crackers.

Laila finishes the joke and sits back up, utterly straight-faced, as if nothing at all had happened. Lipschitz, though, cannot control himself. The joke is funny, and he can feel himself beginning to laugh. It begins as a slight tickle in his throat, then the tickle grows, swells, like a bright red balloon in his chest that threatens to burst at any moment.

Lipschitz runs for the door, trying to contain his laughter until he gets outside, but he bumps into a waitress as he goes, upsetting the serving tray in her hand and causing two orders of nachos and a side of fries to tumble to the ground.

Everyone stops to see what happened, except for Lipschitz, who is scrambling out the door.

The parrot says, "Asshole."

Nobody laughs.

The parrot is being judgmental, and is only considering the man's actions from its own privileged heteronormative perspective.

* * *

Lipschitz returns the following night, and the night after that. Hour after hour he sits beside his beloved Laila, and she whispers funny things in his ear – stories, jokes, observations, none of which can be repeated here for obvious legal reasons.

He becomes quite good at holding in his laughter, and leaving calmly as if nothing afoul is afoot, but sometimes, on the way home, he recalls one of Laila's jokes, and he hears her voice in his head and he feels her breath on his ear, and he has to duck into an alley and bury his face in his coat in order to smother his riotous laughter.

Then, one night, as he returns home, his sister Sophie stops him. She examines his eyes, his face, his countenance.

"What have you been up to?" she demands. "Where have you been?"

Lipschitz feels terror grow in his chest. Sophie is a fiercely devoted activist, with nothing but contempt for the brother who once made his living encouraging people to laugh at breasts and vaginas and penises and gender differences and the elderly with impaired cognitive functional abilities. She

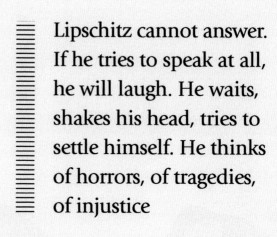

Lipschitz cannot answer. If he tries to speak at all, he will laugh. He waits, shakes his head, tries to settle himself. He thinks of horrors, of tragedies, of injustice

would love to make an example of him and he knows it.

"Nowhere," Lipschitz says.

"Then why is your face red?" she asks.

"It's cold out."

"It's seventy degrees. Were you laughing?"

"I was just running," he says, heading to his room. "It's late."

Lipschitz knows he is playing with fire, but he can't stop himself. His father, abusive and violent, died when he was eleven. His mother became bitter and controlling, his sister foul and resentful. Life went from dark to darker, and humour was the only coping mechanism young Lipschitz had, a thin but luminous ray of light through the otherwise suffocating blackness of his life. He imagined God on Day One, looking down at the world He had created, with all its suffering and heartbreak and death and pain and sorrow, and realising that mankind was never going to survive existence without something to ease the pain.

"Behold," declared God, "I shall give unto them laughter, and jokes, and punchlines and comedy clubs. Or the poor bastards won't survive the first month."

And so Lipschitz, despite the danger, returns to the pub again the following night, and he sits at the bar, beside a Russian, a Frenchmen, two lesbians and a paedophile, and he waits for Laila to show up.

That's not funny, either. Singling out different nationalities only leads to contempt, and homosexuality has no relation to paedophilia.

After some time, the bartender approaches.

"She's not coming," he says.

"Why not?" asks Lipschitz.

"Someone reported her."

Anger burns in Lipschitz.

It was Sophie, he knows it.

Lipschitz turns to leave, whereupon he finds two police officers waiting for him at the door. He is wanted for questioning. He must come down to the station.

"But I'm not going to drive drunk until later," Lipschitz says.

Nobody laughs. Drunk-driving is a terrible crime that costs the lives of thousands of innocent people every year.

* * *

A witness in a Malicious Comedy case – two counts of Insolence, one count of Mild Hatred – is called to the stand.

The witness's name is Lipschitz.

The defendant's name is Laila.

Lipschitz takes the stand, and for the first time in weeks, his eyes meet hers. She smiles, and so great is the pain in his heart that he has to look away. Behind her, in the gallery, sit Lipschitz's mother and sister, the bartender, the Russian, the Frenchmen, the two lesbians, the paedophile, the priest, the two cops, the rabbi and the nun with a parrot on her shoulder.

They scowl at him.

The prosecuting attorney approaches.

"Did you or did you not," he asks Lipschitz, "on Thursday the last, discuss with the defendant the fate of two Jews who were stranded on a desert island?"

The audience gasps.

Lipschitz avoids making eye contact with Laila. If he does, he will laugh, and if he laughs, she will be found guilty. He fights back a smile.

"I did not," says Lipschitz.

The prosecuting attorney steps closer.

"And did she not," the prosecuting attorney demands, "on the Friday following, tell you what became of a Catholic, a Protestant and a Buddhist on the USS Titanic?"

Lipschitz wills himself to maintain his composure.

Out of the corner of his eyes, he sees Laila covering her own mouth, hiding her own smile, and he quickly looks away.

"She did not," says Lipschitz.

The prosecuting attorney slams his fist on the witness stand.

"And did she not," he shouts, "tell you of the elderly couple, one of whom has dementia and one of whom is incontinent? Was there no mention of them?"

Lipschitz cannot answer. If he tries to speak at all, he will laugh. He waits, shakes his head, tries to settle himself. He thinks of horrors, of tragedies, of injustice.

And then it happens.

Laila laughs.

She explodes with laughter, throwing her head back, her hand on her chest as if she might burst from joy.

"Order!" demands the judge.

Lipschitz begins to laugh, too. He laughs and laughs, and tears fill his eyes, and the judge bangs his gavel. He gets to his feet, furious at the outburst, but as he does, he steps on a banana peel and flips, head over heels, to the floor. The prosecuting attorney and bailiff rush to his aide, whereupon all three clunk heads and fall to the ground. Laila and Lipschitz laugh even harder, but the crowd does not. There's nothing funny about head and neck injuries, which can cause cortical contusion and traumatic intracerebral hemorrhages.

"Guilty!" the judge yells as he holds his throbbing head. "Guilty!"

He clears the court, and orders Laila and Lipschitz taken away.

But later, when the bartender, the Russian, the Frenchmen, the two lesbians, the paedophile, the priest, the two cops, the rabbi and the nun meet at the pub, one and all swear they could still hear their laughter long after the courtroom was empty. ⊗

Shalom Auslander is an American novelist, essayist and short story writer. His latest novel Mother for Dinner was published in the USA in September 2020

Poet who haunts Ukraine

STEPHEN KOMARNYCKYJ introduces work by writer **VASYL STUS** and explains why, long after his death and the end of the Soviet Union, his prosecution and imprisonment is still causing political uproar

NEARLY 35 YEARS after Vasyl Stus died in Soviet labour camp Perm 36, a new book about the Ukrainian poet's prosecution and trial has been censored.

Stus was prosecuted for speaking out against repression in the Soviet Union and his poetry was prohibited. He spent five years in a camp from 1972 to 1977 and two years in "internal exile" in Magadan, 11,000km from his Ukrainian homeland.

He was then sentenced to 10 years in a labour camp in 1980 for "anti-Soviet activity" because of his membership of the Ukrainian Helsinki Human Rights Union. His defence lawyer during that trial was Viktor Medvedchuk, who is now an influential Ukrainian politician and friend of Vladimir Putin.

Many Ukrainians blamed Medvedchuk for Stus's death. In 2019, journalist Vakhtang Kipiani published a book, The Case of Vasyl Stus, which suggested that he was complicit in the poet's prosecution.

Medvedchuk took legal action, and in October 2020 a Kiev court banned

> To be a Soviet citizen is to be a slave. The greater the ... abuse I endure, the greater my resistance to this system which abuses humanity... becomes

references to him in the book.

Dmytro Stus, the poet's son, says that the title of the offending chapter, Did Attorney Viktor Medvedchuk kill Vasyl Stus? is not a totally accurate characterisation. But Kipiani cites the Ukrainian poet and human rights activist Yuriy Lytvyn who was incarcerated in Perm 36 with Stus and was also defended by Medvedchuk. At the time, Lytvyn said the case against Stus was fabricated and the "passivity" of his defence lawyer Medvedchuk was because of "instructions from above". The comments, originally published in 1981, corroborate Kipiani's argument that Medvedchuk was complicit in Stus's prosecution. Censoring the book will not strike those comments from the record.

Despite the censorship order, the book continues to be printed in its entirety in Ukraine and topped the bestseller lists shortly after the October judgment came into force.

Stus, who died on 4 September 1985, became a hero to many Ukrainians because of his tenacity in the face of oppression. He wrote hundreds of poems during his incarceration. His work expresses the resilience of the individual who finds strength from the simple experience of perceiving the world and he describes Soviet reality with absolute honesty.

His work expresses what Stus saw and felt rather than the aesthetics of Soviet sloganeering. His style ranges from beautiful lyricism to grotesque fables reminiscent of Miroslav Holub.

The KGB reviewer of his first collection, Zymovi Dereva (Winter Trees), described it as the poetry "of decadence and ideological decline".

Stus was as uncompromising in his political views as he was in his poetry

and in 1978 he renounced his Soviet citizenship, saying: "To be a Soviet citizen is to be a slave. The greater the ... abuse I endure, the greater my resistance to this system which abuses humanity... becomes."

None of the four poems below was ever published in the Soviet Union.

Thirty years after its fall, the banning of a book about Stus's case shows that politics still confronts freedom of expression in Ukraine. ⊗

Stephen Komarnyckyj is a PEN award winning translator and poet who runs a small publisher, Kalyna Language Press, and looks after four Bosnian rescue dogs

50(01):90/93|DOI:10.1177/03064220211012314

ABOVE: A monument in Kiev to Ukrainian poet Vasyl Stus on the site where he once lived; TOP-RIGHT: The KGB's photo of Vasyl Stus after his arrest in 1972.

The Sea

The sea
A dark fragment of sadness,
The soul of Mephistopheles
Solitary.
The piano endures
Beneath girlish fingers, falls
Into the water
From the rim of the earth.
The withered grasses
Capture the damp passages
The moan of the elements
Engulfed in fog.

* * *

Evening thickens with a sura from the Koran
A guttural sound streams through the ravine.
How much truth and anguish lie in the throat?
Too much to narrate before the morning.

* * *

The morose crackle in the empty forest
A bird's sharp whistle.
Leaf fall.
Where shall the butterfly settle?

For Vintsas Kuzmitskas

The cold stellar glow of the Priuralsky dusk
Grew. The frost ordered its organ pipes
And the pines truly and symbolically seemed
Like a provincial theatre auditorium
Where, whatever the bogus gestures of the conductor

However many fake notes and profiles are struck
Nothing can drown out the cold-eyed, severe glow
Of Johann Sebastian's cosmos. The night grew
And I grew within it. The winds blew. The frost
    crackled.
The winds blew. The knuckled
Branches of fir trees crackled. One red eye

Of an electric lamp blinked sleeplessly illuminating
    the area. The drowsy orderly
Broke his dream under his boots...
The frost crackled.

                    The store. The Medsanbat.
And in addition to the poor first kit,
Vintsas, our battalion paramedic,
Ascribed to the register between bandages and
    alcohol
Pyramidone, iodine, formidron,
Silent and solemn himself, like a bandage.
The frost crackled. He turned on the lamps,
Crazily and dreaming between the long shadows,
That were like shards of their own arid longing,
And the spotlights on the wall delineated,
Where some old Flemish landscape canvas
                    Came to life.
The soldier's impoverished palette
Darkened with Lithuanian nostalgia,
While Vintsas made an illuminated target
Where Čiurlionis aimed pine needles,
Walking through a forest engraved in darkness.
                    "Speak"
He asked me, "speak!" And some words
About Vilnius, about Taras, about the Vilnia
And Salomeja sighed softly,
A stream slenderly piercing the aperture,
Of this sombre, enthralling landscape.
He was like a god sandwiched between walls,
Hidden in the hermetic store cupboard,
And awkwardly held out his prickly hands,
Where the half-metre Vilnia flowed.
"Tell me," he requested, "about Taras ..."

Gediminas's scream lifted the ceiling,
Grew under the stars. The prickly forest
of Čiurlionis rustled outside the windows
And the coastal "Letuva" murmured
"Like that and not like that" – He cast aside his
    brush,
Warmed his inhaler, approached, turned back,
And went again, silent, in his assault
on the dyke strengthened by Ruisdael.
"The Ural taiga is painfully similar
To my Lithuania. Orenburg. Shevchenko.
And I have so many compatriots here,

→

→ Going all the way to Pechora.
Indeed, because it is the Fatherland.
You all asleep – and, hairy as coils of fibre,
Wound over, over centuries, your dreams
Roam insensate flattened. And your throat too
   grows hairy.
Tell me. Tell me. Speak!"

Winter Trees

They folded their arms and didn't scream
(How could they without moving their limbs?)
But settled within their snowy twigs:
The poplars were unmoved,
Resting, radiant as candles
Whose cold flame
Was thinned and weakened
By the harsh December day
And immersed utterly in their reflections:
Amphorae brimming with the frosted sandy air
Of this Ukrainian Africa.
Each of them was beyond desperation
A hermetically sealed night
Where the branched nerve flails
Against some primal forest
An antenna that frighteningly catches
The repeated patterns of day,
With its radar corona:
The embroidery of a crow's cry,
The clarity of children's laughter
And the round warble of a police whistle
On the corner of Kreshchatyk Street

Untitled

I knew almost for sure
That he had robbed my friends,
Made my mother miserable,
And given the wife tuberculosis,
So I resolved
To pursue him for payback.
"Where are you, my tormentor?" –
I shouted to the whole deserted hall,

In which my tormentor dwells.
And in response the four echoes,
Of my shouts roared off the walls,
Hit the ceiling
And then fell dead at my feet.
"Where are you, my tormentor?" –
I cried for the second and third time,
And my four roars rose from the dead,
Struck the ceiling
And fell dead on the ground again.
"He is really dead?" I decided he was happily.
But when I got home,
I saw stood by my door
Two legs, two arms and a torso
(there was no head).

"What are you doing here?" – I took him by
   surprise.
And, afraid, those two arms, two legs and a torso
Composed themselves into a headless corpse.

I grabbed that decapitated body without a head,
And shouted into the neck's empty hole:
"Tell me, where is my tormentor?"
"Don't hit me," the hole said.
"Go back to the house where you were earlier.
In the first room people without heads sit,
In the second they are without legs too
In the third without arms,
In the fourth room you will see the torsos,
And in the fifth room, nothing.

"That is where your tormentor dwells.

"However, repeat and repeat endlessly
Everything you want to tell him.
Just don't believe in your eyes
For where he is not, he is."

Translated by **Steve Komarnyckyj**

Vasyl Stus *was a Ukrainian poet, translator,
literary critic, journalist, and an active member of the
Ukrainian dissident movement. He died in 1985*

The freedom of exile

LEAH CROSS talks to **KHALED ALESMAEL** about the life of a gay Arab writer

KHALED ALESMAEL WAS raised in the 1980s and '90s during the rule of Hafez al-Assad, father of incumbent president Bashar al-Assad, Alesmael was told from a young age "Don't criticise, don't complain, don't disclose anything, or it will put your family in trouble".

As a journalist, a refugee and a gay man, these words have resonated throughout Alesmael's 15-year career, which began when he took part in children's radio programmes. In 2005, he became a founding member and programme director at Syria Tomorrow, one of the country's first private radio stations, and has since reported on events in the Middle East for a number of international channels.

"Journalism is my passion, my love, my work, it's everything. But as a journalist you are a target, especially in a country like Syria," he said.

After the civil war broke out, Alesmael fled Syria to escape persecution by extremists, and he is now a Swedish citizen. In 2018, he published his first novel, Selamlik, which tells the story of a queer refugee's experience through a homoerotic perspective, set against the backdrop of civil war in Damascus.

"As much as I loved being a journalist, I escaped to the media of art and music," he said. "I felt like it's easier not to suffer."

Cited as the first gay novel to come out of Syria, Selamlik follows Furat who, like Alesmael, is a queer refugee driven by a need to tell his story. "It's a novel, it's fiction, but it has a lot of me in it. I consider myself the best friend of the protagonist," said Alesmael.

Although not an autobiography, Furat's story mirrors Alesmael's own experiences, from the underground freedom afforded by invisible meeting places for gay men in Damascus, to

asylum accommodation in Åseda, and the unexpected restrictions brought with the shift in cultures.

Syria is a challenging place to be a journalist, but stories of queer refugees are also overlooked in the West, where "the narrative is all about families and children". Alesmael seeks to remind people to disregard sexual identity, and that LGBTQ people "lost as much as you did in this crisis and deserve the same things".

"I always wanted to talk about this subject," Alesmael told Index. "While writing in newspapers and magazines I always wanted to write gay stories, but couldn't as I didn't want to put my family in any trouble. In Syria you have your whole family to think of. The regime doesn't threaten you – they threaten your family, your mother, your sister."

Since the outbreak of the civil war in 2011, Syrian society has become more tolerant of LGBTQ people, if only because the general concerns for necessities such

as safety, water and food trump such societal prejudices. However, the threats he faces remain real, and Alesmael hails from a culture which systematically rejects his themes. Getting published – either in Arabic or English – is a challenge faced by many queer Arab writers.

Yet in his writing, running alongside these turbulent experiences, is a playfulness. Alesmael juxtaposes Arabic and Western cultures in a way that seeks to educate the ignorant and challenge those who choose to be homophobic.

His story for Index, At the Gents' Room, balances humour and romance with the awkwardness of impromptu sexual encounters and seeks to confront those who might be disposed to shy away from the issues he explores. ✖

Leah Cross is senior events and partnerships manager at Index

50(01):94/97|DOI:10.1177/03064220211012315

ABOVE: Still from the film Mr Gay Syria about gay Syrian refugees in Europe

At the Gents' Room

A FEAR OF police. A feeling I did not acquire but inherited from my father – just like his dense, black beard, his wide nasal tip and his stocky, hairy body.

I speed up my pace in my sneakers and my eyelined eyes are chasing me in the mirrors at the departure lounge of Heathrow airport. I have to search for him in each mirror. We agreed that our eyes must not meet. I can't phone him or even text, he has blocked my number for his safety.

In the crowd, two policemen are stopped by an old lady who seems to be asking for information. One talks while the other scans the lounge. His hunter green eyes meet mine. The policeman has a neat, thick brown beard and his body is well built; a pistol protrudes from its holster above his chunky buttocks. As much as I am terrified, I want him to say something to me. I hardly take my eyes away from him. I look up at the flight schedule screen above him and check the time of the flight to Riyadh.

Two hours remain and yet he does not show up. The numbers are flashing in red, and I am looking for him among the many black beards as no mirror reflects him. I walk through the lounge, trying to hide from the two policemen. I hear his voice in every Arabic word said around me, but he is not there. I go chasing amber perfume in the hope it leads me to him.

I stop in the centre of the lounge and take my mobile phone out of my pocket and unlock it.

His name, Ahmad, appears as the first name in my contacts list. I ask the name: "Where are you? Are you backing out of the plan?"

The policemen are passing by me. I return the phone to my pocket and leave the crowd and lean on a wall closing my eyes and praying to Allah in my heart to find him.

I open my eyes and find Ahmad wandering among the travellers in his bright-white thoub, pushing a luggage cart with his thick arms and sunglasses covering his eyes. Behind him, there is a black burka hiding a person inside who is seemingly short, full-bodied and holding the hand of a young ponytailed girl. The girl is carrying a pink box with a doll inside it. I look at Ahmad again and he is still wearing sunglasses. I don't know if he sees me.

He frees his hands from the cart and sits on the edge of a bench and leaves space next to him. The girl approaches him first and puts the box on the bench, sits down and invites the person in the burka to sit next to her.

He puts one of his legs on top of the other and replaces his foot in a leather flip-flop on his knee, showing his big toe. He picks a small handbag from the top of his luggage pile, opens it and takes out a green book. He hands the book to the girl and it turns out to be a Koran as the girl kisses it and puts it on her forehead three times before she opens it while waving her legs in the air.

He, in his sunglasses, looks at the open Koran in the girl's hands as he's also reading. The person in the burka pulls the mask up and reveals another mask, but with an opening that shows eyelined eyes. I am afraid she is his wife. She covers the girl's head with the tip of her mask while burying her head in her handbag searching for something.

Ahmad eventually takes the sunglasses off and puts them in his chest pocket and his eyes meet mine. Alhamdulillah The two policemen pass by and block his eyesight as my heart races with panic and my fingertips freeze in fear.

A rosary bead of red agate stone passes between his thick fingers like a small snake. He rises from his place, turns his back on me, talks to his wife, points his finger to the right then walks.

I follow him as the student follows a teacher, indifferent to where he takes me and what the result is, as if I am under the influence of anaesthetic. Taking my heavy steps and ➔

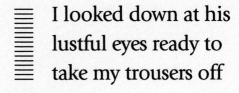

I looked down at his lustful eyes ready to take my trousers off

→ remembering his words that lie in my ears:

"As soon as you see me pointing my hand towards a certain direction, I walk and you follow me."

I follow the scent of oud and amber that he leaves behind him. I pray in my heart that Allah helps us to do it peacefully. He enters the toilets, I slow down my steps and follow.

"Allah, I seek refuge with You from all offensive, evil deeds and evil spirits," I murmur as I enter the bathroom with my left foot.

He stands before the mirror, washing his hands. I stand next to him and look at his face in the mirror, but he ignores me and concentrates on his hands. I must stay at one of the sinks until he calls me. "Ta'al," he says in a gravelly voice. I come closer to him, he puts his hand in his chest pocket as if he is taking something out, and his sunglasses fall out of the pocket and on to the floor. I immediately go down and grab them and hand them to him. He strongly holds my hand with his to take the sunglasses. When he is about to approach my hand with his lips, the policeman enters the gents' room.

Three months ago, I met Ahmad in Edgware Road at a grocery store on a sunny autumn afternoon. He had big black eyes and a chubby body in his white thoub, standing behind the cashier and carrying a packet of cigarettes and some cash. I was not sure if he was following me after I left the shop, but I desired it. I changed my direction and went towards Hyde Park to see if he was walking behind me, and he was. I sat on a bench under a tree and waited for him to join me.

"Assalamu Alaikum." He sat down next to me and initiated a conversation in Arabic as he was sure that I would understand him. With a Saudi Arabian accent, he said that he was in London with his little daughter accompanying his ill wife. I prayed to Allah she would get well soon and I introduced myself as a new Syrian student in London. He smiled when I mentioned my home and passionately spoke about his love for Damascus, and his longing to visit the hamams again as he used to before the war. He put one of his legs on top of the other and placed his foot in a leather flip-flop on his knee, showing his big toe,

and the edge of his thoub got lifted and revealed the bottom part of his hairy thick leg. He looked at me and smiled and I smiled back at him.

He asked me if I knew if there was a gents' room in the park, and before I answered, he said that he would be free for the whole evening and would love to do something to get rid of all his stress. He said that he was tired of being in hospitals for months. He said that no one had invited him for tea at home since his arrival, so he followed and he asked me if I lived nearby. I looked at his leg again as he lifted his thoub and showed more of his leg.

As soon as we entered my student's apartment, he turned his back to me and placed his cheek to the back of the main door. I besieged him with my arms and cupped his big chest with my hands and pushed his body with mine. I inhaled the amber odour on his skin and kissed the nape of his neck and reached his warm ears and licked them. I took my jumper off and glued my bare chest to his soft silky thoub. He turned his face towards mine and swallowed my lips with his hot mouth. I closed my eyes and let him pass his inflamed tongue through my neck, chest and stomach while he kneeled down and I let him open the zipper of my jeans. I looked down at his lustful eyes eager to take my trousers off. I asked him if he still wanted to use the toilet and grabbed him by the hand and took him to the bathroom. He pulled my hand towards his lips and started kissing it and sucking my fingers while I was trying to take his thoub off with my other hand. He left my hand and unbuttoned his thoub and revealed his hairy chest and said that he could not show more. I took off my clothes piece by piece, throwing them at his feet and knelt down, licking his legs and gently pulling the hair with my lips until I felt the hot splashes of my semen falling on my thigh, like silk.

Now I am standing alone in the gents' room at Heathrow airport looking at the chunky bottom of the policeman while he is peeing in the urinal, and inhaling the amber that Ahmad left in the room. ⊗

Khaled Alesmael is a Syrian-born journalist and author. His first novel Selamlik was published in Swedish in 2018

PICTURED: A mural by the Fearless Collective and the Arab Foundation for Freedoms and Equality's Tayf programme in Beirut, Lebanon. The writing reads: "I hear your silence"

Forbidden love songs

Iranian singer **GELAREH SHEIBANI** speaks to **BENJAMIN LYNCH** about living in exile because of her voice

GELAREH SHEIBANI CANNOT go back to her homeland to visit her sick father for fear of arrest.

He is suffering from Alzheimer's disease, and while the 35-year-old would like to return to Iran to see him, the risk is too great.

Although she sees her mother, sister and brother when they visit her in Turkey and other neighbouring countries, she added: "My father is sick, he cannot travel and I haven't seen him for eight years."

Now living in Istanbul, the singer was part of the underground music movement in Iran before she was arrested in 2013. She left not long after to pursue a living making music abroad and continued to release songs online.

"When [the arrest] happened, my father's Alzheimer's started," she said. "I remember how scared he was."

Through choked tears she added: "I was looking at him and thinking maybe this is my fault for creating this pain."

At that time, Sheibani did not think she was leaving Iran forever, and could not have foreseen that she would never see some of her family again.

It was her brother who called her to warn her about grievances held by the authorities back in Iran.

She recalled: "They took my brother and they asked him, 'Why is she still doing this?'

"He called me and told me, 'Don't ever think about coming back to Iran'."

Musicians often draw on their experiences, and My insight – the extract provided to Index and reprinted below – is

no different. Such a feeling of pain and longing for home naturally bleeds through into the lyrics written by someone who uses music to express herself.

"This song has layers for me," she said. "After I was arrested I went to China and I started to perform there. I was signed to some agencies. It was very difficult for me because I had to work, I had to make money because my family couldn't support me, I had to just start doing whatever I could.

"I was in north China, I didn't know anybody, I was so homesick. I had very bad depression, I was thinking about all the things that happened – the courts, how my dad felt, how they were scared for me. It was so crazy, and I missed them a lot."

Sheibani's crime in the eyes of the Iranian authorities was, quite simply, her voice. Her songs were not political, but the very idea of her singing was an affront to a theocratic Islamic government that deemed her – or any woman's – singing unlawful, for fear of inciting lust in men.

The cause of the problem was her audience. Women can sing to crowds in Iran, but it must be either as part of a choir or to a female-only audience.

Her music videos contain powerful and moving images, relating to the songs with colourful and expressive pictures. They are, in some ways, empowering.

But this form of expression drew anger from the authorities.

Iran boasts some of the world's most renowned, respected and beautiful art and poetry, and expression through art is ingrained into its culture. The censorship

of music stems from an argument about its place in Islam. During the 1979 revolution, Supreme Leader Ayatollah Ruhollah Khomeini said: "Music is like a drug. Whoever acquires the habit can no longer devote himself to important activities. We must completely eliminate it."

Though not eliminated completely, music-making continues to be strictly controlled.

In August 2020, the previously imprisoned musician Mehdi Rajabian was arrested again for working with female singers and dancers. It is incidents such as this that make Iranian artists and musicians fearful.

Sheibani believes it's musicians who suffer the most under such controls.

"In other types of art, [such as] in acting, they have some activities they can do," she said. "This is my sound; it is my voice. I can influence with my voice [and] it is forbidden."

Though it was decided Sheibani's singing was a challenge to Iranian authorities, she insists it was not her intention to provoke.

"My songs were about love; they weren't something going against the government. Nothing political," she said. "But it had a different sound. It was different for them to hear this new sound for a new generation. From the beginning [this government] are limiting women in any way they can… they're really against the freedom of women. They don't count you as human, they don't want you have a voice, to talk, to have value.

"Definitely they are scared of women having a voice or an opinion, an idea." ⊗

Benjamin Lynch is editorial assistant at Index

He called me and told me, 'Don't ever think about coming back to Iran'

50(01):98/99|DOI:10.1177/03064220211012316

My insight

Missing you so much
In these lonely nights
Why our hands
have fallen apart?

You there and me alone
Its the bitterness of these moments
On our way
A limbo of arguments

You could fall in love with me
you were afraid of it
You knew I could fall for you
You chose to ignore it

You feared my vision
You feared my voice
You feared my flame
And you realised
I couldn't sleep... without you

You feared my pride
You feared my past
You feared my lonely heart
Told you I was struggling...
   with the world

You there and me alone
It's the bitterness of these moments
On our way
A limbo of arguments

REVIEW

Firestorm

Film: Collective
Director: Alexander Nanau
(Romania, 2019)

A FIRE AT THE Bucharest nightclub Collectiv in 2015 killed 26 people, with a further 38 dying in hospital. The hospital deaths occurred as a result of bacterial infections caused by watered-down disinfectant, and led to the uncovering of corruption and malpractice that brought down the Romanian government.

It is a tragedy that deserves well-crafted and empathetic storytelling. Collective provides this but does not get stuck in an endless stream of grief and despair, with director Alexander Nanau electing not to focus too greatly on the heartbreak of the families.

Instead, Nanau manages to invoke another emotion – anger – and captivates his audience through following the teams of journalists working on the revelations that eventually brought down the government.

Anger is key to its story. For events such as the Colectiv fire, where justice is not given to families and victims, sadness is an underlying emotion. A lasting fury can exist as long as the injustice that fuels it does, and following the journalists who relentlessly work to break the shocking stories of corruption and greed that caused the deaths of 64 people show that rage manifested on screen.

Its hero and protagonist is journalist Cătălin Tolontan, the editor of a sports newspaper, while the newly appointed health minister Vlad Voiculescu gets to grips with the corruption in which the government is mired.

There is no commentary. Nanau could have been guilty of brash, in-your-face and overstated outrage, but the pain of the fire and the subsequent revelations were dragged out over many months, so a slow, chronological tale is chosen. Commentary is not needed when the journalists' investigations tell the story so well.

The horrors of the injustice are carefully teased out. When sometimes

ABOVE: Journalist Cătălin Tolontan who revealed the corruption and appalling conditions that caused the deaths of Romanian hospital patients

the documentary threatens to be slow, the audience is suddenly jolted awake through cases of shocking inhumanity. Scenes of maggots living in the heads of the victims due to improper hospital treatment are sickening – but necessary. It is hard to imagine that this happened in a modern European country.

It is a well-produced and enthralling tale, and a unique film. But one thing is all too familiar.

As Tolontan says during the film: "When the press bows down to authorities, the authorities will mistreat the citizens." ⊗

Benjamin Lynch is editorial assistant at Index

It is hard to imagine that this happened in a modern European country

REVIEW

Bees and flies

Film: The Dissident
Director: Bryan Fogel
(USA 2020)

THE CENTRAL EVENT of The Dissident – the brutal murder and dismemberment of journalist Jamal Khashoggi in the Saudi Arabian embassy in Istanbul in October 2018 – is one of the most horrifying political assassinations of the 21st century.

Khashoggi had become a thorn in the side of the Saudi regime, which was desperate to represent itself as modernising and reformist under the de facto leadership of Crown Prince Mohammed bin Salman.

Khashoggi, via a column for The Washington Post and direct activism with other dissidents, was undermining Saudi propaganda on a daily basis.

A year earlier, according to The New York Times, bin Salman had made it clear he was going after Khashoggi "with a bullet".

The government of US president Joe Biden has now released a CIA report that concludes bin Salman personally ordered the murder.

The problem for Khashoggi, as Bryan Fogel's documentary makes plain, was

not so much that he was a dissident (although that was bad enough) but that he had once been a loyalist. Indeed, Khashoggi had spent many years acting as an informed and articulate voice for a moderate vision of Saudi reform: nuanced, at times critical but always arguing that the desert kingdom needed to reform from within at its own pace.

Everything changed for him during the Arab Spring of 2011 when he realised that people across the Arab world, especially the young, were impatient not for reform but for revolution.

The Dissident is an admirably clear and utterly necessary piece of filmmaking. It explains how 59-year-old Khashoggi had allied himself with the next generation to fight "the flies", legions of online trolls employed to target bin Salman's opponents. With Omar Abdulaziz, a young dissident video-blogger based in Canada, Khashoggi

ABOVE: The fight for justice goes on for Hatice Cengiz, the fiancee of Jamal Khashoggi

began to fight back with an online army of his own, known as "the bees".

This film is also about Abdulaziz, who blames himself for the death of his friend and mentor. If Khashoggi had not yoked himself to the hopes and desires of the younger generation he would never have become the dissident of the film's title and would probably be alive today.

Questions remain about why a man of such experience took the decision to enter the Saudi embassy that day. The answer is probably the simplest one: he was careless in desperation to obtain the paperwork to marry his 38-year-old Turkish fiancée, Hatice Cengiz, and forge the ultimate alliance with the younger generation. ⊗

Martin Bright is editor at Index

 ## This is an admirably clear and utterly necessary piece of filmmaking

REVIEW

Silencing abuse

Film: Athlete A
Directors: Bonni Cohen
and Jon Shenk
(USA, 2020)

THIS SHOCKING DOCUMENTARY uncovers the manipulative world of elite gymnastics in the USA. It documents the verbal, physical and sexual abuse of young girls who were following a dream to become the best in the world.

And it lays bare the lengths to which the governing body of the sport went to hide what was happening when those girls tried to get their voices heard.

It is uncomfortable viewing because it makes us confront the difficult truth that all of us who have enjoyed Olympic gymnastics were watching abuse in plain sight. We see footage of very young gymnasts wincing and then smiling painfully as they land on broken feet and cracked vertebrae and are then made to perform again on the same injuries. They were called names by coaches because of their weight.

These girls, the film alleges, were chosen not only because of their youth, talent and flexibility but because they were young enough to be easily controlled.

In the 1950s and 1960s, retired elite gymnast Jennifer Sey reminds us, grown women competed in gymnastics competitions, but that had all changed by the 1970s and was solidified in 1976 when 14-year-old Romanian gymnast Nadia Comăneci won the Olympic gold medal. Her coaches, Bela and Martha Karolyi, who had been part of dictator Nicolai Ceauşescu's system, then went to the USA and used the techniques they had perfected behind the Iron Curtain to train young American girls.

At the centre of the documentary is Larry Nassar, the team doctor who was the only person the girls trusted, who was kind to them and left them sweets on their pillows at training camp. He also sexually abused them.

One girl, Athlete A, Maggie Nichols, complained in 2015. She was dropped from the team and it took years for her to get justice. Eventually, as the film documents, hundreds of girls came

ABOVE: American gymnast-turned-whistleblower Maggie Nichols, also known as 'Athlete A'

forward to say the same happened to them, and Nassar was imprisoned.

Despite everything, little has really changed. At the end of the film, Steve Berta, the then investigations editor of the Indianapolis Star, which first broke the story, describes a situation where a girl was told by USA Gymnastics that if she continued to complain about her coach she would be off the team, regardless of her performance.

"That system is still in place today," he says. "They are clinging to a process which has been used in the past to silence dissent." ⊗

Sally Gimson is an associate editor at Index

50(01):100/102|DOI:10.1177/03064220211012317

 These girls were chosen because they were young enough to be easily controlled

LEFT: The BBC Beijing bureau office on 12 February, the day after China revoked its licence

END NOTE

War of the airwaves

IAN BURRELL looks at why the UK's media regulator banned China's state broadcaster CGTN, and the battle for global news domination

SET IN SHINING offices beside a lake on a landscaped business park, the new London hub of China's state broadcaster was seen as a major stepping stone in its global ambitions.

Employing 100 journalists, the new editorial powerhouse at Building 7, Chiswick Park – handily placed for Heathrow airport – was to be CGTN's launchpad into Europe. It would dovetail with newsrooms in Beijing, Washington DC and Nairobi so that the network could "follow the sun" in providing 24-hour global news coverage in English with a distinctly Chinese perspective. "See the difference", it implored audiences in its marketing.

Then, on 4 February, less than 18 months after the launch of this London production operation, CGTN was off the air as UK regulator Ofcom stripped it of its licence.

Yet the Chiswick Park newsroom continues to operate beyond Ofcom's reach, hosting an hour of programming

every day as CGTN streams 24/7 to UK audiences via its website, a YouTube channel and internet TV platforms such as Apple TV, Roku and Amazon's Fire TV without the need for a licence.

Even so, the repercussions of the regulator's decision have been profound. In a tit-for-tat response, Beijing blocked BBC World News from broadcasting in China. The channel, already limited in Chinese reach to international hotels and embassies, had been found to "seriously violate" broadcasting guidelines, according to China's National Radio and Television Administration.

China also removed the BBC World Service from RTHK, Hong Kong's public broadcasting platform. Research by the Australian Strategic Policy Institute found that the Chinese Communist Party ran a disinformation campaign on Facebook, Twitter and YouTube early this year to undermine the BBC's reputation at the time the broadcaster was revealing its investigations into systematic rape taking

place in internment camps in Xinjiang.

The row has focused attention on the intense competition taking place in global TV news. For decades, the BBC and CNN dominated this sector, but in recent years there has been a stampede of state-backed entrants to the field.

Qatar's Al Jazeera led the way, followed by diverse outlets including Press TV (Iran), France 24 and TRT (Turkey). The current ecosystem pits public broadcast models such as Germany's Deutsche Welle and Japan's NHK World against expansionist state-sponsored models including CGTN and the Kremlin's Russia Today (RT), which pursues an obvious editorial agenda of criticising the West.

According to Richard Sambrook, former director of news at the BBC, "not everybody can tell the difference" between a broadcaster that receives public funds to report news independently and services controlled directly by their governments.

He said: "The rule of thumb is 'Can it bite the hand that feeds it?' The BBC will often be critical of the British government, but you will never have criticism of the Chinese government from CGTN or the Kremlin from Russia Today, or even much of Qatar from Al Jazeera."

Some new players are awash with cash which they use to buy reach in lower income countries. "They pay to play," said Peter Horrocks, a former director of the BBC World Service who recently joined Ofcom's content board. "The normal model in broadcast TV is [that] someone pays you for your channel. In this world, especially with the money that [channels such as] Al Jazeera and the Chinese bring to it, it's about paying local networks to carry the channel."

Amid this fierce competition, regulators have a tough job distinguishing between impartial news and state propaganda, and if they do take punitive action they can →

Ofcom found the channel in serious breach of impartiality rules over its reporting of anti-Beijing protests in Hong Kong and issued a fine of £225,000

→ be cast as enemies of free speech.

Responding to Ofcom's ban, CGTN issued a statement complaining that the regulator had been "manipulated by extreme right-wing organisations and anti-China forces".

Hugh Goodacre, an economics lecturer at University College London, wrote on CGTN's website that the UK authorities were "taking measures to prevent people [in the UK] from having access to information and understanding of countries that do not unquestioningly submit to the wishes of the US and other Western countries".

But that's a long way from reality.

CGTN's licence was revoked not because of the content it broadcast but because it would not separate itself from the Chinese Communist Party. Ofcom is required by the 2003 Communications Act to ensure broadcast licences are not held by those under political control.

The regulator spent more than 10 months negotiating with CGTN in order that the channel might restructure

ABOVE: The top floor of Building 7, the home of CGTN Europe at Chiswick Business Park, London. The site was sold to Chinese investors in 2019

its ownership model after it became apparent that its licence was wrongly held in the name of Star China Media Limited, its distribution company.

Ultimately, CGTN would not declare itself independent of CCTV (China Central Television), the domestic broadcaster in a one-party state.

Shutting CGTN down was not Ofcom's motivation. That much is clear from its treatment of Russia's RT, which has a shocking record in twisting the news.

In 2019, the regulator fined RT £200,000 for seven breaches of impartiality rules in covering the Novichok poisonings in Salisbury. In retaliation, Russia's media regulator, Roskomnadzor, began investigating the BBC.

RT is state-controlled and funded from the budget of the Russian Federation but continues to hold an Ofcom licence in the name of TV Novosti, a non-profit organisation set up to run the channel. It is part of an array of global news players overseen by a regulator that is required by statute to prioritise news plurality and freedom of expression.

Much of CGTN's London output is anodyne business news. But Ofcom found the channel in "serious" breach of impartiality rules over its reporting of anti-Beijing protests in Hong Kong and issued a fine of £225,000 on 8 March. The regulator also upheld complaints by two individuals whose allegedly forced confessions to Chinese authorities were shown by CGTN. Ofcom found they had been "unfairly treated and had their privacy unwarrantably infringed".

Rebecca Vincent, of Reporters Without Borders, has little sympathy for CGTN's loss of its licence, saying that China was building an "authoritarian model of

information control" on a global scale.

"We wouldn't view Ofcom's decision as an example of censorship, you have to view it in the context of the broader efforts of promoting disinformation," she said. "China is not the only one [culpable] but is doing it in a far more dangerous way than most other states."

Paul Lashmar, head of journalism at City University, said there was a "real battle at the moment going on between partisan news and the notion of impartiality".

And Jamie Angus, director of BBC World Service Group, claims China and Russia have a deliberate "game plan" to create a false impression of equivalence between their state-run operations and the BBC. But he believes the BBC's model, with its "open and accountable complaints procedure" and absence of government interference, makes it distinct.

"These things are fundamental as to whether a broadcaster is genuinely independent or whether it is state-owned and operated," he said.

Ofcom is a light-touch regulator and its deliberately loose interpretation of "due impartiality" allows for a diversity of voices. GB News and News UK TV, new players in the UK domestic market, hope to exploit this flexibility to target conservative audiences which they believe are under-served by existing networks.

CGTN, meanwhile, is seeking a licence in France, where there is no statutory prohibition on political control. Under the terms of the European Convention on Transfrontier Television – which the UK signed up to post-Brexit – the Chinese channel, if successful, could again broadcast into UK living rooms. Any content complaints would need to be directed to the French regulator, the CSA.

Global news has become a high-stakes game and the players will not readily leave the table. ✪

Ian Burrell is a columnist for the i-paper, writing on media

50(01) :103/104| DOI :10.1177/03064220211012318